Seven One-Act Plays by Holberg

SEVEN ONE-ACT PLAYS BY HOLBERG

TRANSLATED FROM THE DANISH BY

HENRY ALEXANDER

WITH AN INTRODUCTION BY

SVEND KRAGH-JACOBSEN

1950

PRINCETON UNIVERSITY PRESS, PRINCETON, NEW JERSEY

FOR THE AMERICAN-SCANDINAVIAN FOUNDATION

NEW YORK

London: Geoffrey Cumberlege, Oxford University Press

Printed in the United States of America
by Princeton University Press at Princeton, New Jersey

CONTENTS

Introduction

INTRODUCTION

Ludvig Holberg's comedies, Hans Christian Andersen's fairy tales, and Steen Steensen Blicher's short stories are the chief pillars in the structure of Danish literature, and a common feature of these three writers is that their genius appears even in their slightest works. Their fame, national as well as international, naturally arises from their most important work, but even in their less significant products there is a suggestion of greatness. The seven one-act plays that Professor Henry Alexander presents to us here exhibit this quality in the great Danish dramatist.

Holberg's greatest works are his comedies, which constitute perhaps the proudest chapter in the golden book of Danish literature, but it is obvious that his fame does not depend on these one-act plays, nor do they clearly show his full importance. And yet in this modest portion of his extensive and impressive production there is so much of the genuine Holberg that it is surprising that a Canadian should be the first to think of collecting these one-act plays into a book as a sample of the Danish maestro's art. In their present form they enter the Danish Foreign Office with a friendly greeting from The American-Scandinavian Foundation, following the two volumes of longer plays by Holberg already presented in an English version by this body. And if we examine them more closely, we shall see one feature added to another, until we have a miniature of Holberg and his comedy that is not at all inadequate—although in one respect it fails: it cannot, naturally, give us an idea of the scale he works in, which in his main comedies measures up to the standards of world literature. For this the seven full-length plays, already translated in the same series, must be studied.

Note: Mr. Kragh-Jacobsen is Master of Arts (1934) in Danish and French. He has written several books and is now chief dramatic critic of the *Berlingske Tidende.*

The plays presented here follow Holberg's career from the time when in his eager youth his dramatic inspiration broke forth, down to 1753, a year before his death in his house in Kannikestraede in the Copenhagen Latin quarter, on a cold night in January. These one-act plays also show us the enormous variety in the Holberg drama. There are suggestions of Molière's comedy of character and the pictures of manners in the English *Spectator* and its followers. We detect the influence of the Italian *Commedia dell'arte*, which Holberg had got to know during his youthful visits to Paris and Rome, as well as the popular Roman comedies, in which he was always interested. Even the former professor of philosophy can be seen here in these dramas, as in his old age he turns back to his beloved theater. We get a glimpse of the Copenhagen middle class as well as fashionable provincials, and each play gives the impression of the dramatist impelled by his irrepressible desire to write. The native of Bergen who had become a professor in Copenhagen was driven by true inspiration. In his enormous mass of writing—about twenty thousand printed pages—we feel how everything is easy and natural; he never blotted a line. In his most important field, the drama, he is one of the greatest names in European literature.

Ludvig Holberg was thirty-five, a professor at Copenhagen University—first in metaphysics, then from 1720 in Latin literature, and after 1730 in history and geography—and already a well-known historian, when he was inspired by a poetic "raptus" and began to write verse—satiric verse, first and foremost the comic epic *Peder Paars*. Already in this first piece of belles lettres we can see the dramatist who emerged a few years later and became the creator of Danish comedy and, in more than one field, the pioneer in Danish literature.

A good deal was happening in the capital Copenhagen during those years; what is most important for us was that the idea of a theater was realized. It was in the air; there was a great desire for a Danish stage—a place where the national tongue could be heard instead of the court actors' French or the German of the market-square buffoons. When the plan was started, it received support from the highest quarters. Frederik IV, the absolute monarch, had dismissed his French court actors, but their leader, René Magnon de Montaigu, married to the daughter of a Copenhagen court confectioner, had not the courage, after thirty-five years of activity in the Danish capital, to return, middle-aged and poor, to his native land. Capion, the organizer of places of entertainment, built a theater with all the necessary conveniences in Little Grønnegade, and when the high chancellor Holstein and the first secretary of the "Danish chancellery," Frederik Rostgaard, both related to the king, supported the idea of a theater, everything went smoothly. In a lucky moment about New Year 1722 Professor Holberg was approached, and six months later—even before the theater in Little Grønnegade was opened on September 23, 1722—Holberg had given his first five comedies to the Danish actors. Within a year and a half he had completed his monumental achievement—the fifteen full-length plays that are still the essence of Danish dramatic literature. The theater in Little Grønnegade had five or six years of as varied an existence as any theatrical company had ever experienced. At times there was great rejoicing and the house was so full that the balcony almost caved in. But more often there were great difficulties, and after various crises the theater went bankrupt for the first time in 1725. It started again in 1726, and Holberg wrote once more for the actors, but in 1727 it collapsed again, and this time Holberg put an end to his dramatic activity.

However, a man who has once breathed the delightful aroma of the theater can never forget it; he is like the circus horse who has once danced to music: when the fascinating notes are sounded, he must obey. When the pietistic regime that had been introduced by Christian VI expired in 1746, the capital awakened to a new and gay life under the young, cheerful Frederik V. The actors got busy, and Holberg with them, even before they moved to Kongens Nytorv, where they built their own theater in 1748, on the lot by the side of the Royal Theater, in which in December 1948 their successors celebrated the two hundredth anniversary of the Danish theater with tributes from theaters throughout the world, and with three of Holberg's comedies brought to life vividly on the stage. Holberg, now an old man, supported the foundation of this royal theater, and not merely in a consulting capacity. He once more took up his pen and added six new comedies to his earlier series. It is true that none of these measures up to the brilliant masterpieces of his youth, but none is without signs that it was written by the great maestro of Danish comedy. Let us look more closely now at the group of plays that Professor Alexander has presented to us.

Master Gert Westphaler or The Talkative Barber is part of the first fruits of the Holberg drama, as it is one of the first five comedies already written before the opening of the theater in Little Grønnegade. It is the last play in the first volume of Hans Mikkelsen's comedies; Holberg used the pseudonym Hans Mikkelsen when he published his early satirical works and the three first volumes of his comedies. Even before he produced this comedy about a barber he had depicted a figure like Gert Westphaler. We find him in the third canto of the fourth book of *Peder Paars*, where Corporal Niels tells about "Gert Westphaler who often talks sixteen hours about one word"; that talkative barber had become so unbearable that his chatter had driven Corporal Niels out of doors. Barbers are well known in the world's literature, and the most famous of them all, Señor Figaro of Seville, undoubtedly was loquacious too. But Holberg's character is entirely his own invention and stands out solidly in the play. We may note that *Master Gert Westphaler* was not originally a one-act play, as the first edition of the comedy—the one we know from the first volume of Hans Mikkelsen's comedies—is in five acts, which were, however, soon reduced by Holberg to the one-act play we find here. And in 1816 Knud Lyhne Rahbek wrote a three-act play which included a number of the good scenes that had been omitted, and by so doing gave the actor who played Gert a better part.

The reason for Holberg's reduction of the play from five acts to one act was undoubtedly the poor success of the first performances of the barber comedy. It was not only the other characters in the comedy who could not stand the everlastingly talking barber and ran away from him. The public, too, was bored. They reacted in the same way as the people on the stage. For once the illusion was too great; Holberg notes that some of the audience left the theater before the piece ended. In the one-act version, which he made later from the original text by means of drastic cuts—unfortunately eliminating a few of the best scenes and characters—he got more unity and vigor into the story, especially by making Master Gert's unsuccessful wooing the pivot of the whole plot. The play is a comedy of character, closely related to the first, and one of the most famous, of Holberg's comedies of character, *Den politiske Kandestøber* (*The Political Tinker*, published by The American-Scandinavian Foundation). The talkative Master Gert is a spiritual cousin of the politically eloquent Master Hermann; both are workers, and—when they do not abandon their trades in order to talk—good workers, but they are both possessed by fixed ideas. In the barber comedy there is a suggestion that Master Gert was a politician too, but Holberg has stressed his loquacity and reserved the satire of the ignorant but conceited amateur politicians for the play about the tinker. The play steers a course, even in its title, between the abstract comedies of character in which a vice or weakness is portrayed—"the talkative man" by the side of, for instance, "the weathercock," i.e. the changeable woman, or "the fussy man"* —and the comedies of character that satirize a trade or profession, for instance the tinker or the officer (in *Jacob von Thyboe*). We recognize the technique in Holberg's comedies of this type. He learned it from Molière's great comedies of character. The main character is first discussed by the secondary ones so that we get an idea of the defect he is suffering from. We already know Master Gert and his tendency to talk too much, even before he appears on the stage. Then he arrives, and at once shows his weakness in several scenes; finally the denouement comes, which can take one of two forms. Either the victim is cured by the drastic experience he has undergone and promises to turn over a new leaf as, for instance, Master Hermann in *The Political Tinker*, or else he is given up as hopeless, as in the case of Master Gert. The reason for this is perhaps to be found in the plot, the little love episode. In the course of the comedy another and better suitor for Leonora has appeared, the young and sympathetic distiller, Leonard. In the plot by which he gets the girl we recognize the traditions of classical Latin comedy, in which the shrewd slave—in Holberg the servant Henrik—helps his young master to get his beloved by playing a clever trick on those who oppose the union—in *Gert Westphaler* the girl's father, the chemist Gilbert, and Master Gert, who has already been designated as the future husband.

Thus we see that even in this small one-act play the great European traditions of comedy have been combined: the plot from Roman comedy and the play of character from Molière—together with Holberg's own power of inventing and creating an original character, drawing him at full length with living and realistic features, and surrounding him with equally well-observed secondary figures. Of these we note especially poor Mother Gunild, who even has her own characteristic

* See *Four Plays by Holberg*, Princeton University Press for the American-Scandinavian Foundation. 1946.

speech, the Jutish dialect, and the sweet, patient girl Leonora, who at first submits to her father and receives Master Gert amicably but is gradually repelled by his talkativeness.

The Arabian Powder shows in the first place how quickly Holberg became a skillful dramatist. The little comedy is written playfully, but although the central character again is a monomaniac, the author has not produced a comedy of character. *The Arabian Powder* should rather be included among the social comedies, where Professor Vilhelm Andersen places it, and set among the minor works that deal with the follies of society—in this case scientific charlatanism as reflected in alchemy. Professor Hans Brix in his great book on Holberg's comedies, a work on which this introduction leans heavily, has shown that *The Arabian Powder* probably was suggested by an actual contemporary event. Holberg got the story from the Latin collection in the *Utopia* of Biedermann (written in 1604 but first printed in 1640 after the death of the author, the German Jesuit Jacob Biedermann), a work from which he also obtained some material for *Jeppe paa Bjerget* and *Den pantsatte Bondedreng* (*The Peasant in Pawn*, p. 133). The occasion that called forth *The Arabian Powder* can be found in the Copenhagen paper *Extraordinaire Relationer*, where in October 1723 it was reported that the Chevalier Johan Jacob de Maldini had been summoned to Copenhagen where the king had asked to see samples of his "curious sciences." The eighteenth century is of course the time of the great European adventurers, and the alchemists who claimed they could produce gold were known everywhere —and feared by sensible people. In this comedy Holberg may have wished to warn the public against a pseudo-scientific swindle, and at the same time he takes the opportunity to strike a crushing blow against snobbery and the worship of riches. The main character, Polidor, is possessed by a mania; he is ruining himself and his family with his chemical experiments. But Holberg does not give us any specially interesting or individual characterization of him; on the contrary he works out his plot in the manner of the comedy of intrigue and uses it, among other things, to unmask snobbery in the final big scene, in which he shows us the crowd of people streaming in to offer congratulations and flattery when the rumor goes round that Polidor has manufactured gold. In this scene *The Arabian Powder* reaches its climax and has a character of its own. Otherwise it suggests for the most part a routine performance written to provide a short entertaining comedy for the actors. The most original figure is the swindler Oldfox, who shows surprising qualities; we get the impression of a man who has long since realized the baseness of human beings and knows that the world wants to be cheated —so he cheats to benefit himself, but at the same time with a suggestion of contempt for humanity. Oldfox is a swindler of international dimensions. *The Arabian Powder* appears in the second volume of Hans Mikkelsen's comedies and was first performed in 1724. It was written at a time when Holberg was producing comedies at a great pace.

The same period sees *The Christmas Party* (*Julestuen*), but this play is much more significant and of higher quality. It is his best one-acter and one of his most important social comedies—or comedy of manners, to use the terminology of international literature. Without any sign of conscientious scruples, Holberg stole the subject from a contemporary dramatist J. R. Paulli, who had handed over to the Danish actors an incomplete play *Jule-Stuen og Masqueraden* (*The Christmas Play and the Masquerade*). It was never acted, but somehow Holberg got hold of it and made from it two of his best works—the three-act play *Masquerades*,* which contains the best portrayal of the servant Henrik in Holberg's work, and the one-acter, *The Christmas Party*, with its entertaining picture of a social setting. In his comedy Paulli satirizes social

* See *Four Plays by Holberg*, Princeton University Press for the American-Scandinavian Foundation. 1946.

abuses—the Christmas games that caused all kinds of frivolity—and the frivolous Shrovetide masquerades. Holberg's comic treatment of the same subjects is much richer and really dramatically brilliant. A great humorist has found material that suits him.

The Christmas Party was to some extent a successor of Holberg's most English comedy *Barselstuen*, which was inspired directly by the *Spectator* papers and contains a group of cleverly drawn female figures around an elderly man in an awkward situation—just like Jeronimus in this shorter comedy. In *The Christmas Party* Holberg deals with a bad Scandinavian custom, the old Christmas games, and the tone in this little comedy of manners is characterized on the whole by a cheerful and untroubled paganism. These Christmas games, with their roots in the superstitions and mystic rituals of primitive times, are the culmination of the party, which reflects the life and setting of the Danish provinces and which is conjured forth on the stage in thirteen scenes that with a steadily rising tempo lead to the catastrophe which after the fall of the curtain will cause great alarm in the strait-laced little provincial town with the fruity and fragrant name of Aebeltoft (Applefield). In *The Christmas Party* Holberg shows us a series of types in the house of a rigidly conservative provincial merchant. Jeronimus rules like a monarch over his little world with a paternal hand both strict and mild, and only his rebellious wife Leonora can stand up to him; he is so fond of her that she can, when she wants, wind him around her little finger. We see the solid country superstition in Jeronimus' sister, the faithful Magdelone, and a picture of peasant naïveté in the figure of the simple Karl Arv. We meet a travesty of Latin learning in the schoolmaster, the hypocrite who wheedles his master and makes a fool of the maid Pernille. She is her mistress's intimate helper when Fru Leonora suddenly falls in love with the gallant visitor, Monsieur Leander, and immediately decides—as proudly as any unfaithful Frenchwoman—to cuckold her old spouse, whom she has tired of long ago.

Holberg works out his comedy in a masterly fashion. He constructs character after character with features and qualities that make them living and convincing against a variegated and captivating setting. We meet the black-clothed schoolmaster, his cane raised, at the head of his group of children, whom he ushers in with the oft repeated slogan "Christopher, Henning, Peer, Else, Marie, Anne." We see the behavior of Fru Leonora, a mother of six children and still ready to misconduct herself with a stranger, but the comedy does not hide the author's amusement at the situation and the erotic atmosphere of the Christmas games with its final explosion. The skillful playwright lets the curtain fall while the riotous proceedings are at their height and the watch are dragging the whole Christmas party to the town hall. Holberg has avoided the chilly awakening next morning; his comedy ends with the climax, and when the curtain falls, we still sit and enjoy the gay comedy of manners we have been watching. *The Christmas Party* is a great comedy, even though it is on a small scale, and it is above all a lively play about real people with human desires and human failings.

Diderich Menschenskraek (*Diderich the Terrible*) is another comedy from the 1720's. It is not one of the most important, and Professor Brix is certainly right in thinking that Holberg wrote it to provide the actor who took the part of Henrik with a bravura role. Henrik Wegener was one of the young students who were captivated by the theater in Little Grønnegade, and his talent was so great that Holberg, as a permanent compliment to his young actor, gave the name Henrik to the servant in his plays. In *Diderich Menschenskraek* there is one of these parts for a Henrik, in which the actor is able to show off in his servant's uniform and also in two big scenes in which he is disguised as a soldier and as a Jew, figures that Holberg is fond of introducing into his plays.

In its form and subject *Diderich Menschenskraek* is one of the least Danish of the plays—it resembles both Roman comedy and Molière; we recognize the idea of slavery from ancient times and we find prototypes of Diderich in Plautus's *Pseudolus* and *Curculio*, and elements of the plot are also taken from Molière's *Les Fourberies de Scapin*, which contains both Turks and robbers and other undesirable people. In *Diderich Menschenskraek* it is the rapidity of the action that makes it effective, and it is the clever "slave" Henrik who manages to get Mr. Leander his beloved Hyacinth, whom the swaggering soldier from whose name the bombastic title of the play is taken has acquired by paying a large sum of money. The comedy is certainly good theater; this is shown, among other things, by the fact that it continually attracts theatrical companies. The Dano-French artiste Gabriel Axel (Mørch), who was trained on the Holberg stage, as the Royal Theater in Copenhagen can still be called, later became associated with the greatest figure in the modern French theater, Louis Jouvet, and is now engaged at his Théâtre Athénée in Paris. During the winter of 1948-1949 he successfully produced *Diderich Menschenskraek*, not performed in Copenhagen since 1864, on a Parisian stage, where the old comedy was revived in a luxurious setting and with the *lazzi* (jests) of the Italian *Commedia dell'arte*.

The Peasant in Pawn (*Den pantsatte Bondedreng*) is not a one-act play nor is it one of Holberg's great works, but it has the merit of possessing a principal character whose one significant speech has become a well-known Danish phrase. "Ask my steward" is the poor peasant boy's continual slogan. *The Peasant in Pawn* was first produced at the theater in Grønnegade in the summer of 1726, but was certainly written earlier. Its construction is rather poor, as it falls into two parts that are not too well connected. This is shown most clearly in the character of Pernille, who at first appears as an important person in the plot but suddenly fades out and never plays the part that she is obviously intended to do in the beginning. This lack of unity suggests—and this is Professor Brix's opinion in his commentary—that the comedy was written in one form and then quickly changed for some other purpose. It looks as if *The Peasant in Pawn* was written at the same time as *The Arabian Powder*—the end of 1723. Its theme, like that of *The Arabian Powder*, was taken by Holberg from Biedermann's collection of stories called *Utopia*, a source that he often used. The play was a pure comedy of intrigue, written for the players and as entertainment for the public. But it was not produced at the time when it was written. In the early summer of 1726 Holberg returned from his last long trip abroad and found the theater in Grønnegade once more flourishing after having been closed for a year. The theater wanted a closing play for June 11—there were people in town and the comedies were going well—and so Holberg rewrote the play about the peasant boy and the swindlers, a work that was lying in his desk. Though a little incoherent, it still was a success, even though it was not produced until some weeks after the June season in 1726.

It is useful to compare *The Peasant in Pawn* with one of the great comedies, *Jeppe of the Hill* (*Jeppe paa Bjerget*) which is also derived from the *Utopia*. The main character in both plays is a peasant who for a brief period becomes a great lord and lives in state, but while Jeppe is a real person who takes an active part himself in the plot, the peasant boy is simply a fool who is used by swindlers and schemers. In his new version Holberg has introduced a touch of the Copenhagen theatrical season into his story. He has also taken the liberty of changing the moral from that of the anecdote in the *Utopia*, where the poor peasant boy was actually hanged in the end. The evildoer was punished; in Holberg's play he gets off more lightly. The whole thing has little depth. *The Peasant in Pawn* is just a stage joke but it shows in various scenes the mark of the true dramatist—and the high spot in the comedy, which has kept its appeal as Professor Brix has shown, is the speech, "Ask my steward."

Holberg's first comedy in the 1750's was modeled on Aristophanes' *Plutus*; it has the same title and is called by Holberg a heroic comedy. The next one was an amusing little farce, a gay interlude that is most often produced at the end of a theatrical evening. The subject of *Sganarel's Journey to the Land of the Philosophers*—as this one-act play is called—was taken by Holberg from his own work, for this comedy can best be described as a dramatization of a section of his long story called *Nicolai Klimii Iter Subterraneum*, written in Latin in 1741. Holberg wanted his great satirical and philosophical work to reach the world, and this desire was amply fulfilled. It was quickly translated into Danish, Swedish, German, Dutch, French, and English, and later into Russian, Hungarian, Polish, and Finnish. As late as 1944 it appeared in a new French translation by a young Swiss scholar, who spent the bitter isolated years of World War II doing this piece of translation. Holberg's *Niels Klim* won its place in great European literature together with Thomas More's *Utopia* and Jonathan Swift's *Gulliver's Travels*. For *Sganarel's Journey* Holberg uses the section in Chapter IX, in which Niels Klim during his journey around the planet Nazar reaches "the land of the philosophers." In the one-acter, various philosophical types appear before the Holberg servant, here called by the Franco-Italian name Sganarel; one scene in the comedy is borrowed from Molière's *Le mariage forcé*. The play runs along easily. Sganarel and Leander have bitter experiences as a result of their encounters with the philosophers; they think they are being rescued by the doctor, but discover that they have merely jumped from the frying-pan into the fire. The philosophers' neglected wives help them out of danger, and the comedy ends with the moral stated in a gay refrain, everybody singing with joyful hearts: "Farewell, land of philosophy."

Holberg's comedies of the 1750's include, besides this small one-act piece, *Plutus,* and two larger philosophical comedies for Holberg's *Abracadabra* version of Plautus's *Mostellaria.* In this work of Holberg, the dramatis personae consist only of men, and possibly as a counterpart to this the aged dramatist wrote his last comedy, intended for actresses alone. Clare Boothe's *The Women,* one of the great American successes in lighter comedy in the 1930's, thus had its predecessors much earlier than most of the audience who watched the cavalcade of women suspected. Holberg himself in *Barselstuen* (*The Lying-in Room*) has written a whole series of scenes for women, but this later comedy is the first in which men were completely excluded. After all the philosophizing in the previous play, the elderly Holberg creates a droll little comedy of intrigue in the manner of his younger period. By means of the company of women he puts on the stage, he shows that he still possesses a sense of humor and that his common sense is alive right to the end of his days. *The Changed Bridegroom* is merely a little play about common sense and about someone who has lost this faculty. For this comedy too we can find a topical source of inspiration in Holberg's own time, a phenomenon that has always amused and astonished people in all ages and all places. In Holberg's youth there had been a sensation in Copenhagen when a tailor's apprentice, who had been married for several years and had previously been a ship's cook, and even taken part in a battle at sea, was found to be a woman. Here Holberg could use the theme that a pair of trousers brings a pleasant change among too many skirts, a theme that runs through *The Changed Bridegroom.* The play shows us the elderly provincial lady Terentia, who runs amok and wants to have a young officer for a husband—and opposed to her a bold and cunning Pernille plus an old swindler, Kirsten the marriage-broker, two lively daughters, and finally the *dea ex machina,* a sensible woman who knows how to cure Mother Terentia's fantastic ideas about marriage. The action gets across easily and ends elegantly with some moralizing verses, which can be added as a pendant to Henrik's final words in *Abracadabra*, in which he maintains that "many things can be done without the help of women." Holberg, the old bachelor who had always enjoyed feminine society, gallantly ends his work as a playwright by contradicting his own Henrik with the lines that conclude *The Changed Bridegroom*.

It's not so hard to carry on
  Without a single man,
For girls and women play their parts
  As ably as men can.

There is philosophy in the comedies right to the end, and in their very last words the great dramatist's gay and lively wisdom shines forth, a quality that we find throughout all his work, from his historical and philosophical tomes to his great immortal comedies and even his small one-act plays.

SVEND KRAGH-JACOBSEN

These seven one-act plays b

Danish-Norwegian play

Master Gert Westphaler
or
The Talkative Barber

[MESTER GERT WESTPHALER]

A COMEDY IN ONE ACT

1722

DRAMATIS PERSONÆ

MASTER GERT WESTPHALER, *a barber*
GUNILD, *his mother*
GILBERT, *an apothecary*
LEONORA, *his daughter*
PERNILLE, *his maid*
LEONARD, *Leonora's suitor*
HENRICH, *his servant*
A JOURNEYMAN APOTHECARY
AN APOTHECARY'S APPRENTICE
GOTTARD, *Gilbert's brother*
TOBIAS, *an attorney*
A NOTARY

MASTER GERT WESTPHALER
OR
THE TALKATIVE BARBER

Scene I

(Henrich; Pernille)

HENRICH. Good morning, girlie. I saw you come out of the chemist's. Have they girls there too?

PERNILLE. No, you made a mistake. I'm not a girl, I'm only an apothecary's jar. That's a devil of a question.

HENRICH. If only you *were* an apothecary's jar.

PERNILLE. Why? I suppose you'd smear yourself with it.

HENRICH. I'd certainly try to get my finger in it. But, quite seriously, are you the maid in this house or something else?

PERNILLE. I've something else to do.

HENRICH. Perhaps you're a prescription?

PERNILLE. Yes, I'm an enema. I think you're crazy.

HENRICH. Pardon my jokes. I've got to go in and bargain for my master.

PERNILLE. Who is your master?

HENRICH. Monsieur Leonard, the distiller opposite.

PERNILLE. I know him. He's a nice young fellow. Is he sick?

HENRICH. Yes, he's hurt himself, and nothing can cure him except a prescription from your chemist's shop.

PERNILLE. Have you a copy of the prescription?

HENRICH. Yes, I have.

PERNILLE. Which doctor wrote it?

HENRICH. Doctor Cupid.

PERNILLE. That's a lie. Doctor Cupid went away years ago.

HENRICH. Bad cess to him if he's not here yet.

PERNILLE. Didn't I say you were crazy? Let's see the prescription.

HENRICH. The prescription is called Leonora, the apothecary's daughter. Now d'you understand what I'm after?

PERNILLE. Ha, ha! Perhaps your master is in love with our young lady.

HENRICH. Yes, that's about it.

PERNILLE. Then the poor fellow's to be pitied. The only prescription that can cure him has been promised to someone else, as perhaps you have heard.

HENRICH. Yes, I know that. She's engaged to Master Gert Westphaler, the surgeon here in town.

PERNILLE. But why didn't your master come earlier? He could easily have had her; he's a very genteel man.

HENRICH. He didn't imagine that the apothecary would promise his daughter so soon. He's had his eye on her for a long time but he didn't dare let anyone notice it because she was so young.

PERNILLE. Where was your master born?

HENRICH. In this town.

PERNILLE. That's impossible.

HENRICH. Why?

PERNILLE. Because he doesn't know that most of our ladies don't want to keep their virginity after they are fifteen. I know that.

HENRICH. But is the match quite settled?

PERNILLE. It's settled between the parents, but not the young people.

HENRICH. How long ago was this?

PERNILLE. The parents decided on the match a month ago but Master Gert has not spoken to the lady yet, and so the parents on both sides are very angry.

HENRICH. Was the match made against his will?

PERNILLE. No. He got his mother to propose for him.

HENRICH. I don't understand that. I didn't think he was so shy.

PERNILLE. He's not shy at all. He's really cheeky.

HENRICH. What the devil's all this? He's fallen in love, he's bold, and yet he hasn't spoken to his sweetheart. Perhaps she's cold to him and won't give him a hearing?

PERNILLE. No, not at all. She's pleased with her father's wish and is waiting every day for the young man to make his proposal.

HENRICH. I see you're angry because I was joking at first, and now you are paying me out.

PERNILLE. No, I'm not so spiteful. I'll explain it all to you. Everybody has his weak point, and Master Gert's weakness is to bore good people to death with useless talk.

HENRICH. What can he talk about so much? Does he know such a lot?

PERNILLE. He has three or four subjects. The first is an old bishop in Jutland, called Arius, who was persecuted because of a book he had published. The second is the counts palatine in Germany, the third is the Turk, and the fourth a trip he made from Harslev to Kiel. So that whatever you begin to talk about, in a jiffy he's up to his ears in the middle of Turkey or Germany.

HENRICH. That's a strange weakness.

PERNILLE. Suppose somebody says "It's nice weather today," he will answer: "I had this kind of weather once when I left Harslev." And then he'll jabber away about the whole journey till he's hoarse, so that if you dragged him from the house by the hair he wouldn't stop holding forth about his trip till he had got to Kiel. That's how he starts chattering every time he talks to the lady, so that the apothecary has often thought of telling him politely to go to the devil. But his mother always patches it up again.

HENRICH. But how can your lady be pleased with that? People who talk so much are usually not much good when it comes to actions.

PERNILLE. She's patient and won't disobey her father, especially as Master Gert's a decent boy and a hard worker.

HENRICH. It's a pity the lady's so patient and doesn't break it off with him. That would be a great blessing for my master, for I can tell you he's been almost crazy since he heard she was engaged. But here he is himself.

SCENE 2

(Enter Leonard)

LEONARD. Henrich, who are you talking to?

HENRICH. The apothecary's maid.

LEONARD. Oh, is it true that your lady is engaged?

PERNILLE. Yes, she is, Monsieur.

LEONARD. I've thought about her for a whole year, and now I'd decided to ask for her. But just as I was going to do it I heard a rumor that she was promised to Master Gert Westphaler. I'm sorry, for her sake, because she'll be marrying a tiresome fellow whom everybody avoids because he chatters so much, but still more for my own sake because, in this unexpected way, I am parted from one whom I have long sincerely desired. Henrich, you know how often I have spoken about her.

HENRICH. Yes, I know, and I often said: "Hurry up, Monsieur! Before you know it somebody'll get ahead of you."

LEONARD. Oh, but I thought she was so young.

HENRICH. She's fifteen, Monsieur. Just ask this girl how much fifteen years means these days.

PERNILLE. Monsieur, I'm deeply sorry both for her sake and yours, as I'm sure our young lady would be better off with you. But I see her coming.

SCENE 3

(Enter Leonora)

LEONORA. Pernille, you must go in to Father. But who are you talking to? Oh, it's Monsieur Leonard.

LEONARD. Oh, my dear lady, I get so agitated when I see you.

LEONORA. But why, sir? Do I look so horrid?

LEONARD. No, on the contrary. I wish you *did* look ugly to me.

LEONORA. That's a strange wish. I'd like to know the reason for it.

LEONARD. The reason, dear lady, is— Oh, what's the use of giving you a reason? Adieu, beautiful lady! May all go well with you! *(Exeunt Leonard and Henrich.)*

SCENE 4

(Leonora; Pernille)

LEONORA. What did he mean by that, Pernille?

PERNILLE. It meant: that Master Gert should go to Jericho.

LEONORA. Aren't you ashamed to be so spiteful about my sweetheart in my presence?

PERNILLE. I don't know what kind of sweetheart he is when he stands there talking politics to a young lady instead of making love. I'faith it's not the right kind of talk when you're like that.

LEONORA. I'm sure he'll lose his love of talking.

PERNILLE. Oh, Miss Leonora, it's no use saying that. I believe if you sewed up his mouth, he'd learn to talk through his nose.

LEONORA. Well, let's change the subject. Tell me what Monsieur Leonard was talking about.

PERNILLE. He was quite desperate when he heard you were going to get married. He's been in love with you a whole year.

LEONORA. I wonder how he dare presume to say such things.

PERNILLE. But why are you sighing so deeply?

LEONORA. That's not true. I wasn't sighing at all.

PERNILLE. Heark'ee, now you sighed again.

LEONORA. Pernille, leave me in peace. (*She goes out, holding her handkerchief to her eyes.*)

PERNILLE. I'faith she was crying. I can see that if it depended on her she would take the other one. But I hear the apothecary calling. I must go in.

Scene 5

(Gunild)

Gunild. That Master Gert's terrible. Every day now for a whole month he's promised me to settle the matter. He's been in the apothecary's house more than ten times and had every chance to ask for his daughter. Why, the apothecary himself has brought the girl down to the room to him for that very purpose. But whenever he comes back and I ask him if the match is settled, he answers: "I'll do it tomorrow. Today I got talking so much to some strangers I met at the apothecary's that I had no time to do what I intended." And now the apothecary is quite angry and asks me if I and my son are having a joke with him, as the matter is quite settled between the parents; all that remains is for him to say the word to the girl. But today he's sworn that he'll go through with it. So I'll go ahead to the apothecary and put him in a good temper first. But there he is.

Scene 6

(Enter Gilbert)

Gilbert. Heark'ee, fellows! Take care that everything's in order for when the doctors come. They are going to inspect the shop this afternoon. But I expect that if the brandy and gin are good, they won't bother much about anything else. That's the way Doctor Herman has inspected my shop for the last ten years. The only question he asks is: "Have you any good sal volatile? We must test that, my dear colleague." And when we've emptied seven or eight bottles of Rhine wine the inspection is over. But there's Gert Westphaler's mother. Your servant, Madame.

Gunild. I'm so glad I found you. I've a notion to talk to you.

GILBERT. A notion? The best thing for that is to take senna. But I think I know what you mean. I've said over and over again that I like the idea of being a father-in-law. You promise that your son will come along and settle the matter. He does come, but every time he keeps jabbering away about other things on into the night. I've never seen anyone go courting like that in all my life. But i'faith I'm not going to be made a fool of any longer. If he wants my daughter, he'll have to put an end to it.

GUNILD. He'll put an end to it all right, Mr. Apothecary. It's not that he's cold, you know; he's as much in love as anyone could be.

GILBERT. Then why the deuce doesn't he propose instead of telling us all his tales? What do I care about Dr. Arius? I have enough to do with the doctors and barbers we have now. That man's been dead over a century and a half and is ready to be resurrected. And what does it matter to me how many popes and electors there are? My shop could get on all right even it there wasn't one in the world.

GUNILD. Today he swore he'd settle it all.

GILBERT. That's good, Mother. My daughter will be at home; he can ask for her. I have no time to talk to him because there's going to be an inspection in my house today. Adieu. But let him come at once.

GUNILD. Look, there's my son himself, if you want to talk to him.

GILBERT. No, I've no time. Just tell him what I said to you.

SCENE 7

(Master Gert; Gunild)

GERT. Why did the apothecary go off so quickly, Mother?

GUNILD. Heark'ee, child. I've pacified him this time, though only after a lot of trouble. The man thinks we're having a joke with him. He's not so far off there. You know it's over two months since the match was arranged, and all that was left was to talk to the girl herself, but one day after another goes by with your confounded chatter that's not worth twopence. D'you think anyone wants to know what you did on your trip to Kiel, how many taverns you went into on the way, how many girls' knees you felt in each tavern, and how many pipes of tobacco you smoked? You know there's a lot of people in town who have gone much farther in the world: Anders Christensen has been three or four times to Bordels and Ruin in France, and away off to Trebizond or Cattesund, but he doesn't talk nearly as much about his trips.

Gert. I'faith I don't just tell trifles about my trip to Kiel, how many quarts of ale I drank and how many pipes of tobacco I smoked, but a lot of things that are worth listening to. You can see if they are trifles, Mother, if you'll let me go over the whole journey quickly—

Gunild. Oh, go to Jericho with your chatter! Get off and do your errand or else say right out that you don't want to, so that we can call it all off. Be off at once! *(Exit Gunild.)*

Scene 8

(Master Gert; a journeyman apothecary)

Gert. Yes, I must really go in and settle the matter. But there's the apothecary's journeyman. Your servant, Monsieur, a word with you.

Journeyman. Your humble servant, Master Gert. Are you going to our house?

Gert. Yes, I want to speak to your lady. Aren't you the journeyman at the apothecary's?

Journeyman. Yes, Monsieur.

Gert. But I haven't seen you long at the house.

Journeyman. No, I've only been helping there for a week, but I worked for nine years in a chemist's shop in Harslev.

Gert. Really, you worked there?

JOURNEYMAN. Yes, do you know Harslev?

GERT. Yes, I certainly know Haderslev. I once went from there to Kiel; I'll never forget that trip. One of the people who was with me was a journeyman hatmaker, a decent sort of fellow who's still living in Kiel and is considered to be the best master hatter (all the hats I've used for a long time were made by him; his work's as honest and reliable as anyone in Jutland). To make a long story short: we went together to Kiel, each with his own trade, to try our luck there. Kiel's a very good town for a man to get on quickly. I know many of my friends who went there with empty hands and in a few years were rolling in money. It's like this: there aren't many workers, and the people in the town are well off and pay plenty. Besides you get good value there. I'll tell you quickly the prices of food when I was there: first, you only paid a Lubeck halfpenny for a pound of the best pork that any decent man would be glad to put in with his peas.

JOURNEYMAN. Oh, Monsieur, it will take too long to tell all this.

GERT. Next, only a farthing for a pound of beef.

JOURNEYMAN. Oh, but this has nothing to do with the trip.

GERT. Third, only four rix-dollars for half a barrel of butter.

JOURNEYMAN. Heark'ee, I tell you straight out I've no patience to listen to all this.

GERT. Fourth, only a Lubeck halfpenny for twenty eggs.

JOURNEYMAN. Eh, what have I to do with your eggs, butter, and pork?

GERT. Fifth, for a quart of French brandy only— Oh, Monsieur, don't be so impatient! Well, I'll leave that out and go on with the journey. In the first tavern on the road we found a man who looked very smart, with silver buttons on his coat and black velvet trousers. This same man was very friendly and said to us, "Gentlemen, won't you have a drink with me?" We thanked him for the honor he did us and drank one tankard after the other with him *in bona charitate* until we were (saving your presence) half drunk. Then at last he suggested we drink like brothers and call each other *thee* and *thou*; we bowed and scraped and drank a brotherly toast with him. Only the coachman sat in a corner smiling. We asked him once or twice, "Coachman, why are you laughing?" But he always answered, "Oh, it's nothing." At last, when our new drinking brother had gone, we found out he was the hangman of Schlesvig. Now I ask you is it fair to blame us for this when, in the first place— Pardon me, I have such a terrible cold, I must turn my head away a little. *(Meanwhile the journeyman sneaks off. Gert speaks and coughs alternately after he has turned away.)* In the first place, I say, we didn't know, of course *(he coughs)* that it was the hangman of Schlesvig *(coughs again)* and then (*coughs again*) if we had known (*coughs again*) it would have been all right, for when you think about what an executioner is *(coughs again and then turns round)* he's just the means by which the authorities exercise their power. But where did he get to? Did the devil run off with that fellow from Haderslev? Hi, Monsieur Harslever! Hi, brother Harslever! What cheek to run away like that when a decent man's talking? I'll certainly tell the apothecary what polite journeymen he has. That fellow must be one of the Haderslev Venetian nobles, he's so tricky. I don't know how it is, but I'm unlucky in this town. If I lived in another place, I could earn money by talking. I don't think that anyone, not even my enemies, can say that I ever start gossip or that they've heard me talking about the weather or marriages or lying-in rooms. I only make speeches, about politics and foreign countries, that you can't find in books and that are worth their weight in gold. But someone will say: why do you throw your pearls before swine? Why do you waste precious words on people who have donkey's ears? I answer: when I begin a speech I must finish it. That's my nature. Nothing annoys me more than when someone hears the beginning of my speech and won't stay till the end. But, zounds! I'm forgetting my errand. I must knock at the door.

Scene 9

(The apothecary's apprentice; Master Gert)

Gert. Your servant, Jesper. Is the apothecary at home?

Jesper. Yes, he's at home, but you can't talk to him; all the doctors are here today.

Gert. What's going on?

Jesper. They're having an inspection. My master told me to call the young lady when you came, Master Gert.

Gert. Good! Tell her I'm waiting for her here.

Scene 10

(Leonora; Master Gert)

Leonora. Your servant, Master Gert.

Gert. Your humble servant, Mamsel. I'm afraid I've come at an inconvenient time.

Leonora. Why?

Gert. I hear there's an inspection today.

Leonora. That doesn't affect me. When Mother has an inspection I'm busy. But this one is only for the men.

Gert. I heard there was as much noise and racket in the parlor as if they were holding a diet or a precinct meeting.

Leonora. What's a precinct meeting?

Gert. I'm very glad you asked me about that, Mamsel—

Leonora. But don't bother to tell me about it just now.

Gert. Because I know as much about it as anyone in this town.

Leonora. I'm sure you do, but I'd rather wait till another day.

Gert. My dear lady, you must distinguish between a German diet and a precinct meeting.

Leonora. I'm sure you must. A German diet is sauerkraut.

GERT. No, that's not right. I'll tell you first what a diet is. A diet is summoned by the seven electoral princes.

LEONORA. That may be, Master Gert. I haven't the honor of knowing any of those good men.

GERT. There are seven electoral princes all together.

LEONORA. So I notice.

GERT. Three are churchmen and four laymen, so the laymen are one more.

LEONORA. I'm so sorry for the churchmen. But what can I do about it?

GERT. The first is the Archbishop of Treves—

LEONORA. He may very well be.

GERT. Then there's the Archbishop of Cologne—

LEONORA. But, Master Gert—

GERT. The third is the Archbishop of Mayence—

LEONORA. Is that possible?

GERT. It's as true as I'm standing here, Mamsel. What would be the use of telling you a lie?

LEONORA. It wouldn't be any use to tell me either lies or the truth about things like that.

GERT *(holding her)*. These seven electoral princes rule over the fourth monarchy. There have been three already, the Phrygian, Elamite, and Mesopotamian, and this is the last. When the electoral princes fall, the world will come to an end too, according to the Sibylline oracle, so they're very careful, as soon as one electoral prince dies, to choose another straight off, so that the world won't come to an end, and this has gone on continuously from the time of the Emperor Augustus, the famous emperor who founded the fourth and last monarchy at the request of the Sibyl, who advised him to base it on the seven pillars. Then that same great emperor did two famous things: first, he levied taxes on the whole world and, second, he established the seven electoral princes. The pope was against this and said: "Your imperial highness, why d'you make so many lay princes all at once?" But the Emperor

Augustus, who was a man who didn't like to be interfered with, got mad and answered: "Your papal excellency, because I want to." Then the pope fell at his feet at once and asked pardon, and this humility affected the emperor so much that he allowed him to make sixteen cardinals all at once, and they are like clerical counts or barons; the cardinal's office goes only to the eldest son, but never to the daughter, so if a cardinal dies and only leaves a daughter, the cardinalate goes back to the pope again.

LEONORA. I've no time to listen to you any more, Monsieur. We'd be very glad if you'd visit us more often, especially if you can come when I'm not at home. And I'll ask you to tell the rest of the story to my cat, for she understands it as well as I do. Goodbye.

GERT. I'faith that was plain speaking. I see I'm getting disliked in this town because of my talking. I swear I won't open my mouth again; the people here are not worth it. You are hated just because you do something they ought to love and respect you for. I must go home and tell Mother what a poor reception I got. *(Exit.)*

SCENE II

(Gunild; Leonora)

GUNILD. Now I must go and find out how Gert got on. There's something strange about the lad. He likes the family, he's in love with the girl, she likes him, the parents have paved the way, he's been on the point of proposing so often, but he never gets there. I hope it hasn't been the same this time too. But there's Mamsel. Your servant, my darling daughter-in-law.

LEONORA. That title doesn't fit me at all. You're just joking with me.

GUNILD. Why? Hasn't Gert been here as he was asked?

LEONORA. Yes.

GUNILD. And I hope he did what he came to do.

LEONORA. I can't deny that. He'd made up his mind to come here and tell me about the German state and what sort of government they have in Germany. He did this so well that I can't complain except that he talked too long.

GUNILD. Didn't he say anything about being in love?

LEONORA. No, Madame. All the time he was talking to me he was on the other side of the Rhine and was getting deeper and deeper into Germany, and I was so afraid I'd soon be taken to Turkey that I had to run off and ask him to tell the rest to my cat. But here's Father; you can hear what he thinks about it.

SCENE 12

(Gilbert; Gunild; Leonora)

GILBERT. Madame, you must pardon me if I speak quite bluntly. From now on I don't want either you or your son in my house, as we don't intend to be made fools of any more and our house to be the talk of the town.

GUNILD *(crying)*. Oh, Mr. Apothecary, I can't tell you how deeply this affects me. I admit that when my son gets started on his old talk he forgets everything he's supposed to do. But apart from that weakness there's more good than bad in him. He's gentle, he's careful about money, he never gets drunk from one year's end to another, he never gambles, he's a hard worker—

GILBERT. I admit all that, Madame. So I'll be glad for him to mix with my journeymen and give them lectures, but he must keep away from my daughter. She doesn't want to listen to lectures.

GUNILD *(ready to faint)*. Oh, oh!

GILBERT. Good gracious, the woman's ill! Run in, Leonora, and get bottle number three from the fourth shelf. *(She comes back with the bottle and gives it to Gunild to smell.)*

GILBERT. Heark'ee, Madame, don't take it so to heart. What

does it matter if your son doesn't get my daughter? He can always make a good match, you know.

GUNILD. Oh, Mr. Apothecary, please be patient just once more, to stop people talking. Believe me, you won't be fooled any more.

GILBERT. All right, Madame, keep calm. Let him come once more, this time in earnest.

GUNILD. Thank you, sir. If he starts on a wild goose chase again, I won't own him as my son any more.

GILBERT. Goodbye now. *(Exeunt Gilbert and Leonora.)*

SCENE 13

(Gunild; Master Gert)

GUNILD. Oh, what a miserable wretch I am! That son of mine will be the death of me. But there he is. How can a lewd, wicked fellow like you dare to face me? It's crazy of me to take this to heart; I should have given you up long ago. How did you get on this last time at the apothecary's?

GERT. Pretty well, Mother. Only Mamsel was a little too hasty.

GUNILD. You mean she wouldn't sit for hours listening to your confounded chatter. You wicked rogue! *(Gives him a box on the ears.)* Tell me *(hits him on the other side of the head)* why did you go to the apothecary's? Was it to talk politics?

GERT. Mamsel asked me what a German diet or precinct meeting was, so I knew I had to tell her, and you can't do that without explaining about the electoral princes and showing that there are seven all together, three religious ones and four lay ones. So, for instance, the religious ones are the electoral prince of Cologne—

GUNILD *(giving him another couple of boxes on the ear)*. There's a couple of the religious and learned ones to match the one from Cologne. Now will you be quiet?

Gert. Oh, Mother, don't be so angry at me. Please make peace with the apothecary just once more. I promise you I won't keep the young lady talking about other things but will go straight to the point, so that she'll be pleased with me.

Gunild. Heark'ee, Gert. When you see me angry, it's only because I love you. I've already made peace with the apothecary without you knowing it, so go there right away, but remember if you behave again the way you did before, I won't own you as my son any more. *(Exit Gunild. Master Gert goes at once and knocks at the door. Leonora herself comes out.)*

Scene 14

(Leonora; Master Gert)

Leonora. Welcome once more, dear Master Gert.

Gert. Your humble servant, my dear lady. I am deeply sorry I offended you before by talking so much.

Leonora. I forgive you, dear Master Gert.

Gert. I hope you will not be angry with me for it.

Leonora. Not at all. Your good mother has made it up again with Papa and myself.

Gert. I admit, dear lady, that at times I talk too much.

Leonora. Yes, so I've noticed.

Gert. A lot of people think it's a weakness, but there are also some good folk who appreciate it.

Leonora. It's all right, Master Gert, if you don't talk so much at the wrong time.

Gert. But have you really forgiven me my previous offense?

Leonora. Yes, Master Gert, with all my heart.

Gert *(kisses her hand)*. I am at your service, my dearest lady. We who have been abroad often have a kind of disease or obsession, or whatever you like to call it, and we must tell everyone what we've heard and seen in foreign countries, so as to show we haven't always stayed at home.

LEONORA. Have you been abroad, Master Gert? I'faith I never knew that.

GERT. Yes, indeed. I once went from Haderslev to Kiel, and I'll never forget that journey [etc., etc.]

LEONORA. Monsieur, if you don't let me go, I'll give you a box on the ears. *(Exit Leonora.)*

SCENE 15

(Master Gert alone)

GERT. I quite admit I talk too much; I get that from my father. But he never gossiped, nor do I. The good folks here in town will certainly miss me when I'm dead and they'll say: "Confound that Gert Westphaler, but he was a better man than we thought; now he's dead there's no one in the town who can talk so well about foreign parts." Yes, they'll say: "If we could only dig him up from the ground again alive." As long as people are alive no one has any respect for them, but as soon as they are dead, they are sorry. Perhaps it's partly envy. They see when I'm together with people I'm the only one who talks. The others would like to speak too but they can't, and so they don't care to hear me talk. Why does Jørgen the glovemaker hate me more than anyone? Just because, of all the people in this town, he's the one who would most like to get a word in, but he can't talk about politics when I'm there because he knows I'll be ready to argue with him at once, as I understand politics better than he does. I've often noticed that whenever I'm together with him he becomes quite silent, as if he wants people to think he's one of those wise men who say little and think a lot. It's an old trick of some of those fools who know nothing, to put on a thoughtful look and keep quiet when educated people like myself and others are there; and with all their pondering they don't think any more than a horse or a sheep. Am I going to tie my mouth up because of that? No, I'd rather be envied than despised. I'd rather have people say,

"What a wicked tongue that fellow has!" than "That fellow sits there like a stupid blockhead or a rascal without a word to say." But what am I to do about this? I admit I talked a little too much to the young lady. But couldn't she have listened quietly till I finished? Had she to threaten me with a box on the ears? I'm sure the apothecary will want the match broken off now. But he'll have to give me satisfaction. I'll defend myself with the law of the land. *(Exit.)*

Scene 16

(Gunild; Gilbert; Leonora; Pernille)

Gunild. I feel sure that my son has obeyed my orders and at last he's really settled the matter that is so close to my heart. But there's the apothecary coming with his daughter alone. Oh, my whole body trembles with fear, I'm so frightened. . . . Your servant, Mr. Apothecary. Where's my son?

Gilbert. Heark'ee, Madame, I'm not going to abuse you. You're a decent woman and quite innocent of all this.

Gunild. Oh, what's happened now?

Gilbert. Your son has behaved just as he did before. He couldn't say a word about love because he was so busy with that confounded talk about newspapers and politics.

Gunild. Oh, what a miserable woman I am!

Gilbert. Don't take on so, Madame.

Gunild. Will you forgive him once more, Mr. Apothecary?

Gilbert. No, Madame. Still we can be good friends. And of course my daughter can get married. Monsieur Leonard, the distiller in this street, has fallen deeply in love with her. I've no need to force my daughter on anyone.

Gunild. I'm quite sure of that. But, Mr. Apothecary—

Gilbert. But, my dear lady, please leave me in peace from now on.

Gunild. Oh, that son of mine will be the death of me. Oh, oh!

GILBERT. I'm very sorry for your sake, Madame.

GUNILD. But, Mr. Apothecary, it's only a slight weakness that will pass with time. He's so decent in every other way. I never have to complain about anything else.

GILBERT. He can be as decent as he likes. I'm not going to be made a fool of again.

GUNILD. Oh, sir, I ask you with tears in my eyes, just forgive him this once. I swear to you by all that's holy I'll never defend him again. But do this because we've been such good friends.

GILBERT. Madame, I can't find it in my heart to see you so unhappy. All right, Madame. I'll pardon him again, but this is the very last time.

GUNILD. I'faith I'll never open my mouth for him again.

GILBERT. Let him come at five o'clock this afternoon, and the lawyer will be there, so that as soon as he declares his love we can sign the marriage contract. Then everything will be settled.

GUNILD. Now I'm going straight back home to preach my son a thundering sermon.

SCENE 17

(Gilbert; Leonora; Pernille)

GILBERT. Well, daughter, he's not going to play any more tricks on me after this. *(Leonora sighs.)*

GILBERT. Why d'you sigh?

PERNILLE. I'm sighing too, Master, although I'm not going to have him. What else can she do? If you had ten or twelve daughters and had to marry them off because you were poor, I could understand it a little, but—

GILBERT. Just you be quiet, Mamsel. I've made up my mind. Besides, there's really nothing wrong with the fellow.

PERNILLE. I'faith he's a decent, clever lad if he wasn't so crazy.

Gilbert. What's wrong with him except that he talks a little too much? That's a common failing with people in his profession.

Pernille. That's true enough, Master. But he's the champion talker among all the world's barbers. Your daughter, instead of going to the bridal bed, will get a lecture from him at night. He'll spend the nights telling her what's in the papers; that's no use to a young lady. I really believe in a year's time she'll be changed into a newspaper herself. All I can say is that I wouldn't take him unless I'd been unlucky enough to lose my ears, so that he could jabber away without bothering me.

Gilbert. Well, it's no use arguing. I shall keep my promise to his mother. *(He goes into the house.)*

Scene 18

(Master Gert; Tobias, the attorney)

Gert. So you would honestly advise me to take an action against the apothecary, Mr. Attorney?

Tobias. Monsieur, I've never advised any honest man not to take an action, or else I'd be very ignorant of law, just as it would be a poor surgeon who would advise a patient not to be bled.

Gert. But d'you think I can win the case?

Tobias. Don't you want to go to law unless you can win the case? What sort of talk is this?

Gert. Why should I go to law?

Tobias. Monsieur, you may be a good surgeon, but you don't understand the law at all. Doesn't a sick man have a doctor even though he's sure he'll never get well, just so that people cannot say he died without a doctor like a brute beast? In the same way, if you don't bother to go to law, people will say: "What a coward! What a mean fellow! He won't stand up for his rights." On the other hand, if you lose a case honestly, you can say: "I've a good conscience; I did everything I could." Besides this is a case you can never lose.

GERT. But, Mr. Attorney, you haven't heard yet what the case is about.

TOBIAS. You say it's against an apothecary?

GERT. Yes.

TOBIAS. That's quite enough, Monsieur. I'm sure you'll win. Sending an apothecary about his business is just a trifle to me. And even if you lose, you'll lose with honor. What's the case all about, anyhow?

GERT. My mother and the apothecary have arranged a match between me and his daughter. I was over there today to propose to her. But before I could do it, I started on another matter, which has happened to me several times before, so she got impatient and threatened to box my ears.

TOBIAS. If you let that go, you must be a rogue. Trust an honest man like me. I wish your life was at stake and you were going to be hanged, so that I could show you how zealously I would defend you.

GERT. Thank you very much. They blame me here in town for talking too much, but I don't talk nonsense. All I talk about is politics and the news. They ought to pay me for that. The people here only want to eat and drink and play checkers or cards. Well, I like my native country Westphalia. My father has told me that in every street there people get together and talk, and you can't get away from them till you're quite hoarse.

TOBIAS. It's speech that makes us different from the animals. But of course there's a time for everything. When you're proposing, you've got to stop talking about other things.

GERT. That's true enough. But I often get talking like that without wanting to. The young lady started me off. Once she asked me what a precinct meeting meant in Germany, and another time about my trip to Kiel, which she thought I explained at too great length. But isn't there time for this, Mr. Attorney?

Tobias. There's not much to say about a little trip to Kiel.

Gert. Isn't there? Oh, yes, there is. I'faith it was a remarkable trip. I left Haderslev on the twentieth of February three years ago, if I remember right—

Tobias. Yes, Monsieur. I don't want to know anything about it. I've been to the Kiel fair a good many times myself.

Gert. No, when I think about it now, it was the nineteenth of February—

Tobias. There's no time to talk about it now. We must discuss the case.

Gert. One of the people who went along with me was a journeyman hatter—

Tobias. You must serve notice on the apothecary at once before sunset.

Gert. No, listen to me for a little while. That hatter was a good fellow—

Tobias. The charge must be laid like this—

Gert. He's still living in Kiel and they think he's one of the best hatters, for . . . (*The attorney goes on speaking while Master Gert keeps talking about his journey.*)

Tobias. Whereas Seigneur Gilbert, an apothecary of this town, has agreed of set purpose to marry his daughter to me, but whereas the said daughter has with contempt turned me out of her house and without reasonable cause wishes to cancel the match, and, as the whole town knows I am engaged to her, my reputation will not allow me to swallow this contempt, but I hasten to assert my rights and to seek the support of the authorities in this case, for if such a thing is allowed, from now on any woman can ruin an honest man's reputation. (*Master Gert puts his hand over the attorney's mouth; the attorney gives him a box on the ears; they start fighting and Master Gert drives Tobias off.*)

SCENE 19

(Gunild; Master Gert)

GUNILD. What the devil is all the noise about? I thought I'd find you at home crying over your sins and now I see you in a fight.

GERT. You'd be sorry for me, Mother, if you knew my misfortunes.

GUNILD. Your misfortunes? No, you should say your misconduct. I've just heard how you behaved again the last time at the apothecary's.

GERT. The young lady turned me away with contempt and threatened to box my ears.

GUNILD. You deserved to be chased away from the house with a stick.

GERT. Then I wanted to consult that lawyer to hear what to do about the case. But he seemed to be crazy; I couldn't get a word with him.

GUNILD. You rascal, are you thinking of bringing a case against decent folk that you've made fools of so often?

GERT. Then what shall I do, Mother? I feel quite unhappy.

GUNILD. Go and hang yourself. You're no use alive.

GERT. Oh, is there no way of making peace with the apothecary?

GUNILD. No, you'd better not think of making peace with him or with me.

GERT. Goodbye, Mother. I don't think you'll see me again.

GUNILD (*aside*). I won't tempt him any more. Heark'ee, Master Gert, where are you going?

GERT. Oh, I'm in such despair.

GUNILD. I've made peace once again with the apothecary, but it was hard work.

GERT. Oh, my dearest mother! Can that be true?

GUNILD. Yes, but you can be sure it's the last time. The apothecary has arranged for the notary to be present, and if you behave properly and get the lady to say yes, the marriage contract can be signed at once.

GERT. Oh, Mother, you can be sure I'll be careful.

GUNILD. You can do what you like. I'll have nothing more to do with it. Come along home now. *(Exeunt.)*

SCENE 20

(Leonard; Henrich)

LEONARD. Now you get hold of the maid and find out how things are and if the wedding is coming off at last.

HENRICH. But what good will it do you to know?

LEONARD. Oh, it's surely natural to want to know about something on which all one's happiness depends. Pretend to have some business and go in and see if you can get her out here. *(Exit Henrich.)*

LEONARD. Oh, I might have avoided all this trouble. That's what you get from being modest. If only I had asked for her boldly the moment I fell in love with her, she would have been mine now. But I never thought she'd give her heart to a fellow like that. She does it only to please her father. But no matter how it is, my misfortune is just as great, as I can't have her. But here's Henrich coming back with the maid.

SCENE 21

(Leonard; Henrich; Pernille)

LEONARD. Oh, Pernille, am I doomed or can I be saved?

PERNILLE. Sir, I can tell you one thing, that the young lady is as unhappy as you. Master Gert has been here again, and his stupid chatter was so abominable that her heart is breaking when she thinks of being tied to a man like him. The apothecary got quite mad too and wanted to break off the match, especially when he heard from us that you loved his daughter. But since then, because of the mother's sighing and weeping, he let himself be persuaded to try once again and arranged a meeting between Master Gert and the notary here at five o'clock to sign the marriage contract if he behaves all right.

LEONARD. But will Miss Leonora consent to this?

PERNILLE. She daren't refuse her father, he's a hard man. But she's opened her heart to her uncle, Seigneur Gottard, who's sorry for her and has promised to get Gert to talk politics again. And when that happens, you must be on hand, so that you can ask for her at once when the apothecary gets mad.

LEONARD. But I'm afraid he'll be on his guard.

PERNILLE. If he is, and she sees it's going to be serious, she'll become violently ill so as to stop the marriage and give us time to make another plan. I whispered to the young lady that you were out here; I expect she'll soon be here. There she is with her uncle.

SCENE 22

(Leonard; Henrich; Pernille; Leonora; Gottard)

LEONARD. My dearest lady, your maid has made me happy. She says you've taken a dislike to Master Gert.

LEONORA. That's true, my dear Monsieur Leonard, but I'm troubled with a hard father.

LEONARD. But, dear lady, I hope that if you stand your ground, your father won't force you.

LEONORA. I do not want to make my father angry before I've tried to arrange the affair peacefully. But if that doesn't happen, I'll have to disobey him.

GOTTARD. Just keep calm, little girl. Let Master Gert come, and you, sir, be here at five o'clock, which is not far off. I hope to get Master Gert talking again and make him lose favor, and if that doesn't succeed, we'll think of some other way. I can't deny that I've never approved of this match and that I'd much rather my niece married you, sir. My brother thought the same too. But he's got a fixed idea he mustn't break his promise. Just keep out of the way now and trust to me. We must go in again.

Scene 23

(Master Gert alone)

Master Gert. Now, Master Gert, the question is whether you can stand the test or be a rascal for the rest of your life. I'm sure I can easily stop talking about learned matters for one hour. *(Puts his fist against his mouth.)* Heark'ee, Mister Mouth, you'll be terribly unlucky if you talk about anything but love this evening, and briefly about that. But when I think about it, it's dreadful that a person should be disliked just because he speaks learnedly. Still I must put up with this; all my happiness depends on it. But I hope to hold my own, unless someone makes me talk. I can't deny that when somebody asks me about things that I know well, I get the greatest pleasure in the world to explain them. But I must train myself so as to resist that temptation. Oh, there's the notary. Now's the time.

Scene 24

(Notary; Master Gert)

Notary. Your servant, Master Gert. I've been called here today because of you.

Gert. I know that, Mr. Notary. I've been here a few times already, but I had to go away without doing my errand.

Notary. Why?

Gert. You know, Mr. Notary, that I sometimes read strange books and, when I'm with people, I like to tell them what I've read. Now and then I've got on to things like that in this house when I should only have been talking about love. But I hope to do better this time.

Notary. I'm sure you can restrain yourself for an hour.

Gert. Please Mr. Notary, will you give me a little practice? Pretend to be the young lady and ask me about some strange thing or other, to see if I can control myself. It's so hard for me to hide my talent, especially when someone gives me a reason for talking.

Notary. Very well. Look, I'm the young lady now.

Gert. Your humble servant, my dear lady.

Notary. Your servant, Master Gert.

Gert. This time I come before you trembling.

Notary. Why?

Gert. Because I offended you last time with my long talk.

Notary. Oh, that doesn't matter; you always talk well. But what's the good news, Master Gert?

Gert. Nothing, dear lady.

Notary. Haven't you read the papers?

Gert. I'faith I have.

Notary. Isn't there anything new in them?

Gert. No, except— No, that's true; I haven't read the papers since I went abroad.

Notary. Have you been abroad, Master Gert?

Gert. I once went from Harslev to Kiel, and I'll never forget that trip. There was a hatter with us— *(Striking his mouth.)* Will you be quiet, you brute?

Notary. What were you going to say about the hatter?

Gert. Nothing except that he was a scoundrel, not worth talking about.

Notary. You're doing very well.

Gert. Yes, I think I'll hold out. Will you go in, Mr. Notary, and tell them I'm here? *(The notary enters. Master Gert walks around practicing, muttering to himself and hitting his mouth.)*

Scene 25

(Master Gert; Gottard; Leonora; Pernille; notary)

Gert. Your humble servant, my beautiful lady.

LEONORA. Your servant.

GERT. I come before you trembling this time.

LEONORA. Do you?

GERT. I most humbly ask your pardon for last time.

LEONORA. As my father has forgiven you for that, I must forgive you too.

GERT. I hope you yourself will pardon my error.

LEONORA. I never go against my father's wishes.

GERT. Your kind father and you have both had good reason to be angry with me.

LEONORA. That's true to some extent.

GERT. But, dear lady, it's my only failing. I'm a sober man and attend to my business.

LEONORA. That's true enough.

GERT. I cannot excuse my behavior to you, but I admit it was an error, although in other places it would be held a virtue.

LEONORA. That may be so.

GOTTARD. You good folks are too fussy. I'faith I'd like to have Master Gert with me always, as I love speeches and, as far as I've heard, he doesn't talk nonsense.

GERT. Thank you very much, sir, for the kind thoughts you have about me.

GOTTARD. But what is it that offends people so much? Is your conversation unseemly?

GERT. No one could say that about me. I only talk about learned and strange things.

PERNILLE. I'll tell you, Uncle. Master Gert is a man who has traveled. During those trips you suffer and spend money. The only thing useful about them is that when you come back you can tell about your journeys.

GOTTARD. So you've been abroad, Master Gert?

GERT. Oh, nothing very special.

PERNILLE. Well, I seem to have heard you went to Kiel once.

GERT. That's quite right. A few years ago I went from Harslev to Kiel, and I'll never forget that trip. We had with us— *(He stops and puts his handkerchief into his mouth.)*

GOTTARD. Who was with you?

GERT *(with his handkerchief in his mouth)*. No one.

GOTTARD. Heark'ee, sir, if you only talk about your journeys and tell stories, I can't see how anyone can blame you for that.

PERNILLE. I'faith, nor do I.

GOTTARD. And I'll scold my brother for being offended about it.

GERT. Thank you very much. But, excuse me, I have an errand with the young lady.

GOTTARD. For my part, Pernille, I must say there are certain things in the papers that I'd pay to have explained. I've often read about the Tories and the Whigs in England, but I don't know why no one in all the town can give me any information about them.

MASTER GERT *(who during this speech has been making love to Leonora, pricks up his ears and says)*: I could tell you about them if I had time.

GOTTARD. I'm very doubtful about that, Monsieur, as no one in this town understands it properly.

GERT. Bad cess to you if I haven't it at my fingertips.

GOTTARD. Oh, I have a rough idea about it. I know the Tories are the people who cut off King James's head.

GERT. You're all wrong, Monsieur. It's quite different. But I'll explain it to you later. First I've got to—

GOTTARD. Ha, ha! I can see you don't understand it. The Tories are those who killed the king. I know that, of course, but I wish I knew something about the others.

GERT. No, that's not right, Monsieur. There are four main parties in England: Tories, Whigs, Mennonites and Anabaptists—

PERNILLE *(softly)*. Now the game's won. I'll run for the apothecary and Monsieur Leonard.

GERT *(continuing)*. The Tories are the upper classes, who

always took the king's side and who fought for King James when he had a war in England against the Whigs, who rebelled under the leadership of Cromwell. This Cromwell, called Massaniello in Latin, was the son of a butcher, but he was so successful that he became knight of the garter and generalissimo by land and sea. For he had a deucedly good head on him. Just imagine, Monsieur, he was so clever he could hold an audience, read, write, and dictate four letters all at once. It sounds impossible, but it's as true as I'm standing here. *(At this moment the apothecary comes in, shrugs his shoulders, sends for Leonard, who is married to the young lady while Gert is talking.)* So King James raised him from one post of honor to another. But when the archbishopric of Canterbury became vacant and the king gave it to a friend called Fairfax, although Cromwell had recommended his brother-in-law, he got so angry that he rose up against the king, got an army together that was all made up of Whigs, Mennonites and Anabaptists, beat King James in a big battle, took him prisoner, and had his head cut off that evening. Then the Whigs were on top. The Tories were suppressed and Cromwell was made Protector of England. But after he had ruled for some years King James's son came back, plotted with the Tories and beat the Whigs several times to their dire misfortune, and finally in the last battle my good Monsieur Cromwell was captured and was torn to pieces by four horses. Then the Tories were on top again and they decided to exterminate the Whigs and their followers, the Anabaptists, and the Mennonites. But as there were too many of these, they changed their minds and only forbade them on pain of death to have guns in their houses. That's why there is so much hatred between the Tories and the Whigs and why the Tories always have to hold their thumbs in front of the Whigs' eyes—But, gracious heavens! Here I am talking away again. Where is the young lady?

PERNILLE. She's gone off. She was married to the young gentleman while you were in England, Master Gert.

GERT. What? Is this true, Mr. Apothecary?

GILBERT. Yes, Monsieur, I kept my word and asked you to come here this last time to settle the matter. But as I see that nothing can be done with you, I've given my daughter to this good man who has been in love with her so long.

GERT. Oh, bad cess to you for starting me talking! Mr. Apothecary, can't you change it?

GILBERT. No. Please remember me to your mother. There's nothing for you here, unless you want my maid Pernille.

PERNILLE. Shame on anyone who would have him, Father! I can't be content with just talk.

GERT. But, Mr. Apothecary—

GILBERT. But, Monsieur, nothing can be done about it. The contract is signed.

GERT. Oh, I'll not stay any longer in this town. I'll go off somewhere else, where people respect learning.

GILBERT. *Bon voyage!* Come, let's go in.

The Arabian Powder

[DET ARABISKE PULVER]

A COMEDY IN ONE ACT

1724

DRAMATIS PERSONÆ

POLIDOR, *a man of high social position*
LEONORA, *his wife*
HENRICH, *his servant*
PERNILLE, *his maid*
OLDFOX, *a rogue*
ANDREAS, *his friend*
A JEW
THE LANDLORD OF THE PHEASANT
LEANDER
HIS WIFE
FIVE OTHER GENTLEMEN
FIVE OTHER LADIES
TWO POETS

THE ARABIAN POWDER

Scene i

(Andreas; Oldfox)

Oldfox. This town isn't as small as I thought. There's a lot of fine houses; there must be some rich people living here. But look, I'll be damned if that isn't my old friend Andreas, that I haven't seen for so many years. Andreas! Is that you or your ghost?

Andreas. Oh, brother Oldfox, how lucky to find you here so unexpectedly! *(They embrace, kiss one another, and cry.)*

Oldfox. Oh, my honest friend and true comrade! I'm almost fainting with joy at seeing you. I thought you were hanged years ago. But I see you know your trade; it's no trick to steal, a coarse peasant can do that, but to steal so that you're never caught, I call that knowing your trade.

Andreas. I thank you most humbly for your good opinion of me, brother. It's a great pleasure to be praised by a fine man like you. And I also thank my parents for their good training and their warnings, that have been useful to me wherever I've been in the world, so that I can say, without praising myself, that I was never caught red-handed except once, and I got out of that pretty well, as I didn't lose anything but two of my ears.

Oldfox. Oh, that's a trifle. A couple of ears more or less don't mean much. I see that's why you wear a Polish hat.

Andreas. Yes, of course. So I greet people just like the officers when they go on guard; I make a little bow and bring my hand to my hat. A lot of people say I'm stuck-up because of this, but they're quite wrong. I'm not at all proud. But how have you been living, brother?

Oldfox. Pretty well. I can get on with everyone wherever I go except those damned judges, who every now and then attack my honest name and reputation. A couple of weeks ago I ran into one who had me put in jail but, to save trouble and delay, I skipped out, as you don't gain anything by lawsuits, brother.

ANDREAS. That's quite right, brother. I've noticed too that those justices are nasty fellows who can't leave decent people alone.

OLDFOX. Yes, they're so envious. As soon as an honest man earns a penny they try to get it away from him.

ANDREAS. Virtue is always persecuted.

OLDFOX. Especially by your own countrymen, and so I've sworn never to set foot in my home town again.

ANDREAS. But what are you going to do here?

OLDFOX. I'faith I haven't thought about it yet. I don't want to be idle; idleness is the devil's chance. I've tried almost every trade. In Augsburg I was a medical doctor and practiced for a long time very profitably, until out of sheer envy the faculty brought a suit against me and wanted to get me hanged though I'd done my job so well that none of my patients could complain.

ANDREAS. I can well believe that; I hope they all died.

OLDFOX. Yes, they did, but they got rid of their illnesses. If I'd been rich enough to continue my case against the doctors, I'd have been able to show them what sort of fellows they were, tormenting their poor patients worse than the hangman for years, while I never kept a patient more than three days. There are some rich people in Augsburg who owe all their prosperity to my prescriptions. If I hadn't cured their dear parents so quickly, they'd still be waiting for their inheritance that came to them according to nature's law. I would only have had to produce their testimonials as to my ability to support my case against the other doctors. But I made up my mind to leave the town instead. I wouldn't have anything to do with those fellows. They judge their own cases there, and when you are sentenced to death and then hanged, you can't get out of it, even if you appeal a hundred times.

ANDREAS. You're right there, brother.

OLDFOX. In Nuremberg I was a prophet and earned money for a long time telling fortunes. I had a big reputation at first, as my predictions came off well a few times. But the spirit doesn't always move you in the same way, and I predicted something about the republic that didn't come off, so they wanted to get their hands on me. But it was lucky I was a prophet. I prophesied something about myself—which every prophet can't do. It was that I'd come off very badly if I was tried, so I took to my heels and got away in time.

ANDREAS. I'faith I could have foretold the same thing, although I've never practiced that art.

OLDFOX. In Frankfurt-am-Main I pretended to be a fencing-master; I got a whole lot of pupils and they all paid me. But when the fencing-school was to begin, I thought to myself: "What's the use of these young people learning to fence? They'll only trust to their skill later on; they'll be reckless and run into trouble." So, to prevent this, I sneaked off.

ANDREAS. Did you give your pupils their money back?

OLDFOX. No, brother. I didn't know how to find them in a hurry and, besides, I needed money for my trip. But, so they shouldn't think I was going to cheat them, I borrowed some money from my landlord as well, to show I'd come back again. From Frankfurt I went to Strassburg, where I pretended to be a politician.

ANDREAS. But how did you manage that?

OLDFOX. It was easy. I read a little of Hübner's *Political Problems*, especially the chapter about Strassburg and the cities round about. I said I was a nobleman, put on an honest and serious look, which is important for a politician, and I also criticized all the actions of the magistrates, found fault with everything in the town, and so got myself such a reputation that I was offered a job, but I wouldn't take it unless they paid me a year's salary beforehand. But when I got their money I thought to myself: "You could do something better than sitting with a miserable pen in your hand all day," so I skipped out without saying goodbye, and that must have convinced those who doubted my ability that I was a big politician. In Cologne, where we were together the last time, I acted the part of an astrologer, in London an alchemist, in Antwerp a saint; this last was the most profitable, as people brought offerings to my house as if it were a church, so that I should intercede for them.

Andreas. Why didn't you stay in that profession?

Oldfox. Just when I was standing in the street calling on the people to fear God one of my old friends came along, looked closely at me, burst out laughing, and said to the crowd: "This man that you think is a saint is one of the biggest rogues on earth." But my stock was so high that the people were ready to stone him for blaspheming a saint. Still this frightened me so much that I didn't dare stay in that town but came along here.

Andreas. What are you going to do now?

Oldfox. I'faith I don't know myself what part to act. I'll count my buttons and take up the trade that comes on the last one. *(He begins to count.)* Doctor, prophet, fencing-teacher, gambler, politician, alchemist, astrologer, saint. *(He starts counting again and ends at alchemist.)* Well, I've got to make gold, and you must help me.

Andreas. You can depend on my services.

Oldfox. Heark'ee Andreas, here's a hundred rix-dollars worth of gold, that's been crushed into a powder. You must mix that with something else. You must put up a table in the market and offer this powder, but don't sell it to anyone unless he asks for the Arabian powder. That's all you have to remember. Leave the rest to me. We'll turn the hundred dollars into four thousand. Look, here's the gold; go right away and do as I say, and stay in the market. When I get the four thousand you'll have a quarter of it.

Andreas. Very well; I'll be ready with the goods in half an hour.

SCENE 2

(A Jew; Oldfox)

JEW. *(He speaks throughout in a mixture of Danish and German.)* Your servant, sir. Have you anything to sell?

OLDFOX. No, nothing just now, Ikey. I've just come to town. But when I start work tomorrow you can get some gold, but only if you promise not to tell anyone, or else I'll have no peace. Besides I only make enough gold at one time to last for a month, but if anyone wants to learn the art, it costs four thousand dollars.

JEW. Can you make gold?

OLDFOX. Yes, just a little for household needs.

JEW. Then you could get into the good graces of an important gentleman who lives here.

OLDFOX. What's his name?

JEW. Polidor. He's spent a lot of time and money on it but never got anywhere. He'd be willing to give four thousand dollars to learn the art.

OLDFOX. Is he a decent man?

JEW. A fine man, a learned man, and a great student of science.

OLDFOX. His studies won't help him much in that art. I can teach a peasant almost as quickly as the most learned man; the art needs only a little knowledge and a few small ceremonies that a person must carry out.

JEW. He's been cheated by so many people that he won't believe anyone now.

OLDFOX. He's quite right. The world's full of cheats just now. So I won't ask him to trust me more than anyone else before he sees the samples and is convinced.

JEW. Do you make gold from other metals, sir?

OLDFOX. Oh, I don't go in for rubbish like that. It's not worth the trouble. I can make gold from anything. Goodbye, I must go back to my lodgings.

JEW. Where are you staying?

OLDFOX. Just nearby at The Pheasant. If you come tomorrow, you can get some gold.

JEW. Good! Goodbye for now.

SCENE 3

(Henrich; the Jew)

JEW. That fellow looks honest, but I don't believe him till I see some samples. I must tell Mr. Polidor the whole story. *(He knocks.)*

HENRICH. Who d'you want to talk to, Benjamin?

JEW. I'd like to speak to Mr. Polidor.

HENRICH. I don't think you can talk to him now; it's his bad time, when he has the fever.

JEW. Has he had that fever long?

HENRICH. No, not more than twenty years.

JEW. Nonsense, I saw him just three days ago.

HENRICH. I'm sure he has a fever. When I see a man standing up to his ears in live coals during the hottest part of the summer, I feel he's either crazy or has a fever.

JEW. Ha, ha, now I get your meaning. He's operating just now.

HENRICH. I don't know if he's operating or taking a purge. It looks to me pretty much the same, as all the time he's been trying to make gold he hasn't got enough to buy himself a rope so he can hang himself when he's thrown away all his money on that rubbish. And he won't see anyone when he's busy at this job.

JEW. But he'll see me if you tell him that an alchemist has just come here and he'll show his samples before he asks for any money.

HENRICH. Well, if that's true, you'll be able to talk to him; otherwise if you said to him: "Your house is on fire, someone's attacking your wife, there are thieves in your house," you wouldn't get him away from that business. But this is really something I can talk to him about.

JEW. Then go in at once. I don't know how long he'll stay in town.

HENRICH. He's sitting in the outer room here; I'll shout outside the window; I daren't go in. *(He calls out quietly three times.)* Please, please, Mr. Polidor!

POLIDOR *(from inside).* Who's that scoundrel that dares to call to me?

HENRICH. I've something very important to tell you, sir.

POLIDOR. And I've something to give you a good hiding with that will teach you to leave me in peace another time.

HENRICH. There's a stranger outside who can make beautiful Arabian gold.

POLIDOR. Tell him to wait. I'm coming right away.

HENRICH. Didn't I tell you? That's the only magnet to pull him out.

SCENE 4

(Polidor; the Jew; Henrich)

POLIDOR *(in a dressing-gown with a leather apron in front, and a broad, broken-down hat on his head, a pair of bellows hanging from his shoulder and a pair of tongs in his hand, his face quite blackened with coal).* Where is the man who can make gold?

JEW. I've just been talking to him. He's staying at The Pheasant.

POLIDOR. Will he teach the art to other people?

JEW. Yes, but it's deucedly dear.

POLIDOR. How much does he want?

JEW. Four thousand dollars.

POLIDOR. That's a lot.

HENRICH. It's not much. I'd gladly give him a barrel of gold if I had it. What does it matter if I could make ten times as much afterwards?

POLIDOR. Then you advise me to give the money, Henrich?

HENRICH. I advise you to hang the alchemist and the Jew too, sir. One's a Jew, and I'm sure the other's just the same as the rest of them who have cheated you so often, sir.

POLIDOR. Heark'ee, Benjamin, will you guarantee that he'll not cheat me?

JEW. No, thank you, sir. I only know him because I've spoken to him once; he'll have to guarantee himself. But he offers to show you samples before he asks for any money.

POLIDOR. That's a reasonable offer. You get him here yourself, Benjamin; I don't want him to think I'm anxious to learn the art.

JEW. I'll go to him at once.

SCENE 5

(Leonora; Polidor; Henrich; Pernille)

LEONORA. Good gracious, my dear! You look like the very devil.

POLIDOR. That's what comes of my work, Madame.

LEONORA. You may very well say that's what comes from your work. What other results have you seen from all those years you've been worrying about that confounded nonsense?

POLIDOR. Mind what you're saying, Madame. Don't talk in that way about the noblest profession in the world.

PERNILLE. You're right, sir, when you call it a noble profession; only rich and important people can follow it. It's good for a person's soul too.

POLIDOR. That's going a little too far.

PERNILLE. But I'll prove it to you, sir. Poverty is good for a person's soul; alchemy makes you poor; therefore it's good for your soul.

POLIDOR. Heark'ee Madame, you shouldn't employ such impudent servants.

LEONORA. My dear, Pernille is right, and no sensible person

can blame her. Your own example is sufficient proof of what this profession leads to.

POLIDOR. When it comes, it comes all at once.

PERNILLE. Sure it comes all at once. You'll distill, boil, and cook so long that in the end you'll set the house on fire, sir, and you'll be poor all at once.

LEONORA. You've been working at it for ten years, and if you stick at it for ten years more, you'll have to learn a trade to get food.

PERNILLE. Yes, make matches when you are poor.

POLIDOR. You impudent hussy! Get in to your spinning-wheel; that would be more useful. And you, Madame, go in and sew on your frames and let me alone.

PERNILLE. Madame will sew on her frames as soon as you let her have some of the gold you've made, sir. Since you make so much gold every day we're not satisfied to embroider with silk.

POLIDOR. I believe the devil's got into that girl. If I wasn't such an honorable man— Heark'ee, in a few days I'll stop your talking and you'll see the results of my work. There's a stranger come to town who is going to show me proofs.

PERNILLE. That fellow! He's the biggest cheat in the world.

POLIDOR. Do you know him?

PERNILLE. He's an anti-Christ. Isn't that what they call the goldmakers in Latin?

POLIDOR. You mean an alchemist. Yes, that's a goldmaker. But how do you know he's a cheat?

PERNILLE. Because he's a goldmaker.

POLIDOR. Bad cess to you if you don't keep your mouth shut. Would you call me a cheat too?

PERNILLE. Yes, why not? You are cheating yourself, your wife, and your children. I'll tell the truth if it costs me my life. Listen to me before I go: it would be better, instead of consulting a goldmaker, to send for a washerwoman who could take the coal and dirt from your face, sir. (*Exit.*)

POLIDOR. I won't have that girl in my house any longer, Madame.

LEONORA. Oh, dear heart, you mustn't hold it against her. She's a good, faithful girl, and she says what she does out of pure zeal.

POLIDOR. Madame, please do me a favor by going away for a little while. I want to be alone.

LEONORA. Certainly.

HENRICH. I'faith, here's the Jew coming with the gold-maker. He ought to be ashamed to be able to make so much gold and not buy himself a decent suit.

POLIDOR. Oh, you don't know these alchemists. They all have a modest appearance. Look'ee, Henrich, take the bellows and tongs inside and get me a wig instead of this hat. *(Henrich runs for a wig and puts it on his master's head.)*

SCENE 6

(Oldfox; the Jew; Polidor; Henrich)

JEW. Here's the man, sir. I had a lot of trouble before I could get him to come with me. Now you can talk to him yourself, sir.

POLIDOR. Your servant, sir. I like to meet people in my profession. When did you come to town?

OLDFOX. It's all the same to you whether I came today or yesterday.

HENRICH *(softly)*. That fellow's a bit hasty.

POLIDOR. Yes, Henrich, all great artists are capricious. I'd like to be of some service to you while you are in town, sir.

OLDFOX. Sir, the greatest service you can do me is to save your compliments. What other service could you do me?

POLIDOR. One person can always help another. I mean that as you are a stranger here in town, I can help you to meet some nice people.

OLDFOX. Nice people, ha, ha, ha! Have you such a good

supply of them? I've been all round the world, but I've never met any nice people. I only found one good man in the world. That was my master Albufagomar-Fagius, an Arabian by birth. He was gentle and kinder to brute beasts than one human being is to another. I remember once, when his cat was lying asleep on his sleeve, and the time came for him to pray, he cut off the piece of the coat the cat was resting on so that he should not disturb its peaceful sleep.

POLIDOR. I call that the height of kindness. We haven't people like that. Have you just come from Arabia, sir?

OLDFOX. No, Monsieur, I came from the moon. I don't know what use these questions are.

POLIDOR. You must start talking about something.

OLDFOX. I don't like these preliminaries. If you have something to say, come to the point at once; my time's precious.

POLIDOR. I've heard you're an expert, sir.

OLDFOX. That may be.

POLIDOR. And as I've been following that science for many years, I'm always looking for a chance to speak to people in the profession.

OLDFOX. What did you use as a guide?

POLIDOR. I've read all the best authors.

OLDFOX. The greatest authors are the greatest rogues; they don't know what they've written themselves. I studied in vain for ten years, and I was just as wise the last day as when I began. But the great Albufagomar-Fagius taught me in one hour what I couldn't find in all those years.

POLIDOR. Won't you teach me the art for a fee, sir?

OLDFOX. For six years since I left my master I've not taught it to anyone, as I was forbidden to do so, but six months ago I applied to him and got this answer that you can see in his letter dated the twenty-third of the month Gorael the year 603 after the Hegira. Look at what he writes: *Allabricamo Triel Sluki, Elmacino Eben Alcantara Masaki Gombada.*

POLIDOR. I don't understand Arabic at all.

OLDFOX. It goes on: *Mihynki Caraffa Almanzora Tarif Elbrunadora Alcantara.*

POLIDOR. What does that word *Alcantara* mean? There's a place in Spain with that name.

OLDFOX. *Alcantara* means a sum of money, in European coinage amounting to four thousand rix-dollars. He allows me to take that fee from anyone who learns the art.

POLIDOR. But I suppose you can take less if you wish, Monsieur.

OLDFOX. No. Listen to what he writes about that: *Aitzema cranganor Monomotapa Lacangandaro Mihopi Madagascar rencolavet.*

POLIDOR. I don't understand that. Is he saying that you can't take less than the four thousand dollars?

OLDFOX. Yes, didn't you notice he said *Mihopi Madagascar rencolavet?*

POLIDOR. But suppose out of your kindness of heart you wished to do it for nothing?

OLDFOX. No, he gives a good reason why you musn't do it for nothing. Look at this: *Bramani Muhamed Nadir Elaocombra Caffares Canunor Elcanan.* So if you wish to learn the art, Monsieur, it will cost you four thousand dollars.

POLIDOR. That's a good deal. But may I take the liberty of asking what use the money can be to you when you can make gold?

OLDFOX. I can't do it for nothing because I have written orders from my master and the reason he gives in his letter: *Bramini Muhamed Nadir.* And I can ask you, sir, the same question you asked me: What do a few thousand dollars matter when you can get the money back at once out of nothing?

POLIDOR. Yes, I suppose you're right. But I'd like to say something else if you won't take offense.

OLDFOX. I can guess what it is: you've been cheated by so many people, why should you believe me?

HENRICH. No, my master wasn't thinking as plainly as that.

At least, instead of the word "cheat" he would have said politely "deceive."

OLDFOX. You're right, Monsieur, and I think highly of your caution. I don't ask you to believe me, so I won't ask for the money in advance but only an assurance that it will be paid as soon as you've seen the proofs of my science.

POLIDOR. All right. I'll hand the money to the Jew and he'll give it to you, Monsieur, as soon as I've seen the proofs.

OLDFOX. Good, I'm quite satisfied with that. I must go in and look at your laboratory, if you don't mind.

POLIDOR. Yes, please walk in.

SCENE 7

(Henrich; Leonora; Pernille)

HENRICH. I'd like to know what's happening. I'm afraid for my master's money. But there's the mistress coming with Pernille.

PERNILLE. Henrich, where's the master?

HENRICH. He's gone in for a little while, and when he comes out, he'll be either an emperor or a beggar. He's made a contract with the new alchemist that will make him the one thing or the other.

PERNILLE. Did the goldmaker ask for money to teach him the art?

HENRICH. Four thousand dollars will be handed over to the Jew Benjamin and the alchemist will get them when he's proved his skill.

LEONORA. Oh, I'm trembling all over already; I'm sure it's a swindle.

HENRICH. No, the master was careful enough to ask for samples first, and when the samples are tested, the money will be well spent.

PERNILLE. But it shows he's a cheat when he asks for money.

Why should a man who can make gold ask money from others?

HENRICH. Well, he gave the master a reason for that.

PERNILLE. I don't know what reason he could give.

HENRICH. The reason was this: *Alcantara Aben Ezra Mahomet podolski Scabhalsiaskomai.* The master found that a good reason and I think there's some sense in it.

PERNILLE. What is it in Danish?

HENRICH. I'faith I don't know. Do I understand Arabic?

PERNILLE. You booby, if you don't understand it, how can you find any reason in it?

HENRICH. Well, the goldmaker explained the words to us afterwards: *Spelamdisimo Madagascar hemancino Rencolavet.*

PERNILLE. I'm still just as wise.

HENRICH. I'faith so am I, but it's certain he won't get any money until he's made a few samples. But there they are. We'd better go in, he wants to be alone with the alchemist.

LEONORA. Oh, oh, I feel in my bones that nothing good will come of this. But when I think it over, it doesn't matter; he'll ruin himself in a day or a year; it's all the same.

SCENE 8

(Oldfox; Polidor)

OLDFOX. No, sir, I won't have anything to do with the experiment, so you mustn't have any suspicions. Have you put as much mercury in the pot as I told you?

POLIDOR. Yes.

OLDFOX. Did you boil it on a low fire?

POLIDOR. Yes, everything was done as you suggested.

OLDFOX. Now here's the secret: certain powerful Arabic words that you must repeat three times while the operation is going on. I have them written here if you can read them, sir.

POLIDOR *(takes the paper and reads). Eregamdlug ere Eregardeb go ud re ran.**

OLDFOX. You must kneel and say it three times. *(Polidor repeats it three times.)*

OLDFOX. That's right. Have you put the Arabian powder in the pot too?

POLIDOR. No, you said nothing about the Arabian powder, Monsieur.

OLDFOX. Oh, oh, that's the most important thing. Without that the experiment will not work.

POLIDOR. But where d'you get that powder?

OLDFOX. Those fellows from Nuremberg always have it on the market. It's used for taking spots out of clothes. You can get a good lot for one mark, they don't know its real qualities. Let your servant run over to the market straight away.

POLIDOR. Henrich!

HENRICH. Sir!

POLIDOR. Run over to the market and buy a mark's worth of Arabian powder.

HENRICH. Who shall I buy it from?

OLDFOX. Most of the people from Nuremberg keep it among their other goods. (*Exit Henrich.*)

POLIDOR. Good heavens, who would think that powder could have such virtue?

OLDFOX. Everything seems trivial when you first get to know about it.

POLIDOR. Is there anything else we've got to be careful about?

OLDFOX. No. You can keep the paper with the Arabian words as a treasure, Monsieur; that's the whole secret.

POLIDOR. But when do you put the Arabian powder in the pot?

OLDFOX. It doesn't matter when, as long as it's boiling. Look,

* If each word is read backwards, this is a Danish sentence meaning: Goldmakers are cheats, and you are a fool.

there's your servant coming back. I knew they had it everywhere.

HENRICH. Here's fourpence back, sir. I got a whole handkerchief full for fourpence.

OLDFOX. Come inside now and throw a good handful in the pot. *(They go in.)*

SCENE 9

(Oldfox alone)

OLDFOX. Everything's going well. I'll let him experiment a couple of times more so that he'll be all the more sure. It's quite certain he'll get about ten rix-dollars from the two handfuls of powder he throws in the pot. Then when I have the money, my friend Andreas and I will get out of town and let the gentleman find out where to buy more of the Arabian powder. Ha, ha, ha! It'll be funny when he sends for something that has never existed and gets to know that nobody has ever heard of Arabian powder. I'll get four thousand dollars from this man and yet I'll be doing him a favor he ought to thank me for, as he'll learn such a lesson from this that he'll give up his crazy ideas and leave other people to make gold. And my friend Andreas has earned a quarter of the money; he's done his work sensibly and faithfully. I've known him for a good many years and I know he's as quick as anyone except me, or else I wouldn't have trusted him in this. But here's the gentleman back again.

SCENE 10

(Oldfox; Polidor)

POLIDOR *(embracing and kissing Oldfox)*. Oh, sir, Heaven has brought you here to reward me for my long work and many years of toil hitherto without result. You have proved your skill; you have honestly earned the four thousand dollars, yes, twice as much.

OLDFOX. I won't take a penny more than our contract calls for.

POLIDOR. Oh, this will shut those people up who have always laughed at me and I'll gloat over my enemies and those who've turned their backs on me because they were afraid I'd lose my money and so they forgot all the kindness I had done them when I was rich.

OLDFOX. Yes, sir, that's the way of the world.

POLIDOR. But now I can despise them again.

OLDFOX. No, you mustn't do that, sir. My great master Albufagomar-Fagius recommends to his disciples humility as the most important virtue. You see my character, sir. I could look like a prince if I wished, but that would be going against our charter. That's why people won't believe we know the noble art when we behave like poor folk.

POLIDOR. And I'll obey your instructions too. You can assure Albufagomar-Fagius of that and give him my most humble respects when you write to him.

OLDFOX. You may be sure of that.

POLIDOR. Here's my signet ring, sir. When you give it to Benjamin the Jew, you'll get the money at once.

OLDFOX. Try the experiment once more just to be sure.

POLIDOR. Yes, if you'll wait a little while longer. My wife will keep you company.

SCENE II

(Oldfox; Leonora; Pernille)

LEONORA. Oh, sir, if only I could find words strong enough to thank you!

OLDFOX. My dear lady, your husband is a good man; that's why I have shown him my secret. *(Pernille kisses his hand.)*

OLDFOX. You are too humble, Mademoiselle. And my hand's rather dirty.

Pernille. Oh, no, it's a precious hand, worth more than one kiss.

Leonora. I hope you won't refuse this ring, sir. Wear it for my sake.

Oldfox. No, my dear lady, I can't take any gifts from you.

Leonora. But, sir, I'd look upon it as a token of friendship if you would. Please don't refuse it, I ask you most humbly.

Pernille. Oh, sir, do the lady that favor.

Oldfox. I'll take it so as not to hurt the lady's feelings.

Pernille. Oh, sir, if only I had something to give you! Won't you take this medal that I got from my parents?

Oldfox. It's a shame to take your inheritance.

Pernille. Oh, sir, I won't let you go till you take it.

Oldfox. I'll keep it for your sake and send you one made of gold. But here's the master back again.

Polidor. Oh, oh, I'm so happy I can hardly contain myself. The process has proved itself. I got just as much gold as the last time. Oh, I hope you'll visit me every day as long as you are in town, sir.

Oldfox. Certainly. I may perhaps stay a few months here.

Polidor. Won't you do me the honor of having dinner with me?

Oldfox. No, I won't have any time, but I'll have the honor of having supper with you this evening. I have a few things to do now.

Polidor. Then I mustn't keep you. You'll get the money from the Jew as soon as you show him the signet ring.

Oldfox. I've no doubt about that. Goodbye for now.

Polidor. Goodbye. You have the best wishes of myself and my whole family.

Scene 12

(Polidor; Leonora; Pernille; Henrich)

Polidor. Well, Madame, what have you to say now? Have I ruined your house with my foolish work?

LEONORA. Oh, dear heart, don't blame me for my indiscretion.

PERNILLE. And I ask you, sir, most humbly, to forgive me for being so bold as to jeer at you so often.

POLIDOR. I forgive you with all my heart; only remember another time not to argue about things you don't understand. Well, Henrich, where have you come from?

HENRICH. Oh, sir, is it true?

POLIDOR. Is what true?

HENRICH. That you can make gold, sir?

POLIDOR. Yes, Henrich, it's quite true, but how did you get to know it?

HENRICH. Oh, it's all over the town. I heard it first from the wine-merchant near here. He said seventeen times he hoped to be in my good graces, gave me a big glass of Canary wine and wouldn't take a penny for it, although the greedy brute previously wouldn't give me a glass of brandy before I'd put the money down on the counter.

POLIDOR. That's just the way of the world. As soon as things go well, everyone wants to be friends with you. But I don't understand how the news got round so quickly.

HENRICH. The Jew must have told somebody, and as soon as anybody knows a thing it's all over the town at once. Everybody who saw me in the street hailed me as if I were a count, and Christopher Buttercup, who never looked at me before, bowed so deeply that he nearly fell in the gutter, but i'faith I passed him by just as proudly as he had walked past me before.

POLIDOR. There's a knock, Henrich. Open the door.

HENRICH. It's Monsieur Leander, sir, who wishes the honor of speaking to you.

POLIDOR. Oh, is that so? That man used to despise me.

LEONORA. Henrich, tell him we don't receive people like him.

POLIDOR. Oh, no, Madame, let's behave properly even if we are wealthy. He can come in.

Scene 13

(Leander; the characters from the previous scene)

LEANDER. Oh, my dear Mr. Polidor, I'm delighted to find you so well; I can't tell you how deeply I've been longing to see you.

POLIDOR. I've never noticed it. I've wanted to call on you several times, but you were never at home, and when I've seen you on the street, you never spoke to me.

LEANDER. My dear Mr. Polidor, you do me an injustice. I call heaven to witness that there's no one on earth I have more respect for than you.

POLIDOR. You can save your compliments, Monsieur—

HENRICH. No, sir, I believe Mr. Leander is your friend. As soon as he heard of your good fortune he was so changed that he was ready to burst with affection for you.

LEANDER. I swear by all that's holy that I'm just as I've always been and that your good fortune is not the reason for my visit. I've always preferred you, sir, to all the people I knew and my greatest happiness is to be one of your most humble dependents.

POLIDOR. That may very well be, Monsieur. But now I must leave you; I have something to do. (*He goes in.*)

LEANDER *(kissing Henrich)*. Oh, my dear Monsieur von Henrich, I ask you to be my friend and patron. Won't you?

HENRICH. Why shouldn't I? *Serviteur très-humble. (They kiss each other again. Three more gaily dressed gentlemen come in and embrace Henrich and, with Leander, go in to Polidor. Leander's wife enters and kisses Leonora's apron.)*

LEONORA. Well, my dear lady, why all this great humility?

LEANDER'S WIFE. Oh, gracious lady, can anyone be too humble with a lady of your quality? You are like a bright light to all of us in this town.

LEONORA. But you never thought about me like that before.

LEANDER'S WIFE. I daren't swear in the presence of such a

gracious lady, but if I did dare to swear, I should take my greatest oath to prove that— *(Three more ladies enter and kiss her apron.)*

LEONORA. Dear ladies, let's go into another room. I see that the whole world's coming in here. So we can't stay in the hall any longer. *(Henrich and Pernille remain alone; the three gentlemen enter and pay profound compliments to Polidor, who is inside; one falls on his head, kisses Henrich, and asks to be remembered, before they leave. The ladies do the same and kiss Pernille's hand.)*

PERNILLE. Isn't it nice, Henrich? All those three ladies kissed my hand.

HENRICH. That was more of a ceremony than with me; the gentlemen only kissed me on the mouth.

PERNILLE. This business certainly makes you feel like somebody important.

HENRICH. Yes, who would have thought that an ordinary wench like you would have her hand kissed by stylish women?

PERNILLE. You're right there, and what about a lubberly mouth like yours being kissed by such important gentlemen? But a lot of coaches are stopping here; we'll have more visits. *(Two gentlemen and two ladies enter and ask the privilege of speaking to the master.)*

HENRICH. I don't know if my master and mistress are receiving. But just wait till they come out. *(Henrich arranges them on one side of the room, while two men come in, dressed in black.)*

HENRICH. Who are you?

POET. We're poets.

HENRICH. Good. You came just at the right time. A cat of mine died yesterday, and I'd like you to write some nice verses for it.

POET. Our humble art is at your command.

HENRICH. But what do you want here?

POET. We want to offer some slight verses in praise of the lady and gentleman of the house.

HENRICH. Good. Just stand on the other side of the room till the master and mistress come out. And take your hats off, you dogs! Don't you know what house you are in? *(They take their hats off and stare at the floor.)*

HENRICH *(walking to and fro)*. Heark'ee fellows, how many verses can you make in a day?

POET *(bowing)*. That depends on our inspiration.

HENRICH. Can you find a rhyme for the words Henrich Larsen?

POET. That's pretty hard.

HENRICH. Eh, then you're a couple of rascally poets. Heark'ee, can you write poetry in prose as well?

POET. No, Monsieur, that's unnatural.

HENRICH. What, it's unnatural? Are you making a fool of me, you rogues?

POET. Certainly not.

HENRICH. How many feet are there in a verse? I've forgotten all that pedantry.

POET. That depends on the kind of verse.

HENRICH. Nonsense! Aren't all verses the same length? But how is it you've never honored the master and mistress by writing poems to them before, when they've always deserved the same praise as they do now?

POET. Because we never had the good fortune to know their virtues before?

HENRICH. You mean you never wanted to know their virtues before you heard about their prosperity. If I have any influence with my master, we'll have a poet hanged every day until the whole tribe is rooted out. But here's my master and mistress; now you can hear what they say themselves. *(Polidor and Leonora come in all dressed up.)*

POLIDOR. Henrich, run at once and get me a dollar's worth of that powder, then you won't have to go for it so often.

HENRICH. Certainly, sir. *(Exit Henrich.)*

POLIDOR. What d'you want, ladies and gentlemen? Do you want to talk to me? *(They step forward, bowing deeply and saying they have just come to pay their humble respects and to inquire whether Mr. Polidor had any orders for them. The ladies do the same to Leonora and kiss her apron. The poets step up and offer their papers.)*

POLIDOR. What are these papers?

POET. They are a few modest verses in praise of you and Madame Leonora.

POLIDOR. Heark'ee, all of you. When the world was against me and you thought that my long and futile work had ruined me, you could find no virtues in me, and you despised my house and talked scornfully about me. But now when my work has succeeded and my house is blessed with riches, you can all see now with your own eyes what you couldn't see before with glasses. Now, if I was the biggest idiot, you'd call me a Solomon; if I was the ugliest man, you'd call me an Absalom; if I was completely wicked, you'd think I was a most virtuous man. That's the way of the world. No one is esteemed unless he is lucky. Oh, and as soon as his luck goes, love and respect go too. Don't imagine I'm so simple that I can't see your falseness, for—

HENRICH *(entering)*. Oh, sir, what has happened? Before I could get as much Arabian powder as I could carry, for fourpence; but now I can't buy a single grain of it even if I offered a hundred thousand dollars for it.

POLIDOR. What d'you say?

HENRICH. Wherever I've been, in the market and at the chemist's, they laugh at me and say I've been sent on a wild-goose chase.

POLIDOR. Oh, heavens, what has happened?

HENRICH. I'm afraid, sir, we've been cheated. Everybody says there never was any Arabian powder. But, good heavens, what's the matter with this man? *(The landlord of The Pheasant comes running in, dressed as a cook.)*

HENRICH. Are you crazy, man? How dare you rush like that into a gentleman's room?

LANDLORD. Oh, oh, if the cup hadn't been an heirloom I wouldn't have been so unhappy about it!

POLIDOR. I see it's the cook who lives opposite. See if you can get him home and calm him down. The poor fellow's in a frenzy.

COOK. And if it hadn't got my dear parents' names on it.

POLIDOR. I'm very sorry about this. He's a decent fellow and the best cook in town.

COOK. The spoon's gone to the devil too, and when I look round, I expect I'll find some other things gone.

HENRICH. Heark'ee, Mister Christopherson, how long have you been crazy? *(Aside.)* If I had a stick to threaten him with, he'd be all right.

COOK. You *can* go crazy from things like that.

POLIDOR. What's the matter with you, Mister Christopher?

COOK. A stranger who said he was an alchemist has run off from my house and taken a silver cup and a silver spoon. I trusted him when I heard he'd been in your house, Mr. Polidor. Just before he left he had with him a one-eyed devil in long black clothes.

HENRICH. Did he have a Polish hat on too?

COOK. Yes, and a sort of plaster over his eye.

HENRICH. Oh, we are ruined! That's the fellow who sold me the Arabian powder.

POLIDOR. Oh, oh, I've lost my four thousand dollars. *(The strangers and the poets put their hats on and walk boldly across the floor.)*

JEW *(enters)*. Is the alchemist here? I gave him a jewel when he got the money from me.

POLIDOR. I'm glad you've been cheated too. You brought him here.

JEW. Was he a cheat? Oh, oh, oh, my precious jewel!

POLIDOR. I've got nothing for my four thousand dollars except a little bit of paper with some Arabic words that I'm supposed to read when I do the experiment.

ONE OF THE STRANGERS. Let me see it. I know Arabic a little. Oh, that's not Arabic and never will be. What the devil is it? When I read the last word back to front, it is *fool*. Let's see the first one. Here it is: "Goldmakers are cheats, and you are a fool. Ha, ha, ha!" *(They all go out laughing; the poets bow with their backs to Polidor.)*

LEONORA. Oh, and I gave him my best ring as well!

PERNILLE. Oh, I'm not so sorry about the coin I gave him but because I kissed the rogue's dirty hand.

POLIDOR. Let's go in. We'll go to the country and live on the little property we still have left. I'll never bother about alchemy any more, but leave it to my greatest enemy. It's made me and many other good people poor. I only hope that decent folk will learn to be careful from my example and others like me. *(They all go off, the Jew and the cook crying.)*

The Christmas Party

[JULESTUEN]

A COMEDY IN ONE ACT

1724

DRAMATIS PERSONÆ

JERONIMUS, *an elderly townsman*
LEONORA, *his wife*
MAGDELONE, *his sister*
PERNILLE, *the maid*
ARV, *the manservant*
A SCHOOLMASTER
CHILDREN
LEANDER, *a young gentleman*
LEANDER'S LANDLORD AND LANDLADY
STRANGERS
THE WATCH

THE CHRISTMAS PARTY

Scene 1

(Leonora)

Leonora. Oh, today has seemed like two days. But love is an overpowering passion; it's like a raging ocean—the more you check it and confine it the more violent it becomes. Oh, Leander, it was sad for me when you came to live in this place and I could see every day in front of me the man whose society I cannot enjoy because of my old husband's suspicions. My only comfort is that I can get a few nice letters from him, in which he pours out his protestations, but they are only like oil that adds to the fire and makes me despair. We've plotted to get together a few times, but so far all has been in vain. If there's to be a chance to enjoy the happiness I've waited for so long and to have a private talk with him, it will be at the Christmas party we're holding this evening. Pernille, who knows about my love, is standing in the doorway to tell me when he passes—he usually does so about this time, as we've arranged it by letter, so that we can see each other through the window. I daren't even open the window because I'm so afraid my husband may come along all of a sudden. But this fear and restraint, so far from cooling my love, just adds fuel to the flames. But there they are.

Scene 2

(Pernille; Leonora)

Pernille. Get ready, Madame, Monsieur Leander is just coming; the signal is three loud coughs. Then you can take him into the hall and come to some agreement.

Leonora. Oh, Pernille, I'm mortally afraid to do that. Suppose my husband happened to come along?

Pernille. Leave that to me. As soon as he comes I'll run

in and keep talking nonsense to the old man. I've thought up a whole lot of stories to keep him as long as you need the time to speak to Leander.

LEONORA. But sometimes he won't listen to any talk.

PERNILLE. I don't want to hear any talk from you either. Do you think, Madame, that I haven't thought everything over? I know what sort of talk that fellow will listen to. D'you think I'm going to tell him what's in the papers: that the French regent is dead, that Mir-Vais has taken a beating in Turkey, that the Spanish silver-fleet has come in, that Prince Eudemius has won a victory over the Duke of Vendosme? No, I'll tell him some old wives' tale that he'll take in eagerly. I'll tell him that a calf's been born with a crest on its head and flounces on its legs, and then he'll start at once to moralize and preach about the wickedness of the age, and about finery and showing-off— But I hear Monsieur Leander coughing outside; run out and bring him in; I'll go off to the old man.

SCENE 3

(Leander; Leonora enters leading him. They both stop in the hall.)

LEANDER *(kneeling)*. Oh, my sweetest Leonora, is it possible that after all this long waiting I shall have the happiness to—

LEONORA. Oh, my dearest Leander, get up, we haven't much time for preliminaries. I feel sure of your love. Let's think of how we can arrange matters this evening at the Christmas party. I know your landlord and landlady are invited, but I'm not sure you will be.

LEANDER. If I'm not, I'll invite myself and take no notice of any sour looks. My landlord and landlady will take me along and make the excuse that they couldn't leave me alone at home.

LEONORA. That will do. But do you know anything about our arrangements?

LEANDER. I've never spoken about them. But my landlady

must have noticed something about it. She said the other day: "We'll soon be going to the Christmas party at our neighbor's Jeronimus, and then you'll be lucky enough to kiss the beautiful Leonora's hand." That made me silent, but my silence was caused by excessive joy. Then she smiled and said: "My husband and I have both suspected something; if we can help you, we'll do so with the greatest pleasure." I thanked her and took her into my confidence, for they are people who would give their lives for me and love me more than their own brother.

LEONORA. Well, dear Leander, it's a good thing they are loyal to you and we have them as accomplices. But how can we manage to get together in private?

LEANDER. We must put our heads together and think of a Christmas game that will give us a chance.

LEONORA. But now I hear my husband coming. We must part.

LEANDER. Then I must say goodbye for just now, much against my will. Goodbye, dearest Leonora. You can be sure that—

LEONORA. Oh, Monsieur, I *am* sure. Goodbye.

SCENE 4

(Pernille; Leonora)

PERNILLE. Well, Madame, did you manage to talk to him?

LEONORA. Yes, of course, Pernille. But why did you come back so quickly? I made him go as soon as I heard the door open; I thought it was my husband.

PERNILLE. If I'd thought of it, I'd have waited a little longer. But I'm afraid, Madame, I've made a devil of a mistake.

LEONORA. How?

PERNILLE. The old man became so pious when I told him the story of the calf that had been born that I'm afraid the Christmas game will be called off.

Leonora. If that's so, you played your part very badly. You often cheat yourself when you try to cheat others. But you can soon put it right; just say it was not true.

Pernille. I'faith that won't do. I swore I saw the calf with the crest and the flounces with my own eyes.

Leonora. That certainly was a bad mistake and we're in a devil of a mess. But did he say there would be no Christmas game?

Pernille. No, he didn't say so definitely, but he began to talk about parties and pranks that should be abolished. If he's got that bee in his bonnet, you must persuade him all over again to have some merrymaking.

Leonora. Yes, that's just the right way to spoil the game. No, if he speaks about it, I must pretend to agree with him; when an old man has a young wife, the more retiring he thinks she is, the more liberty he gives her. But I don't think there's any danger; if we had no Christmas game, our old aunt would be beside herself. She sticks to all those ceremonies as if they were her creed. You couldn't get her to eat unless you had the Epiphany lights on the table. But there's my husband; you run off and talk to Auntie.

Scene 5

(Jeronimus; Leonora)

Jeronimus. Easter is coming, and I give you my word that those women's headdresses, flounces, hanging curls are the invention of Lucifer.

Leonora. What's the matter, darling?

Jeronimus. They see one sign after another and yet they're just as crazy.

Leonora. Has something bad happened?

Jeronimus. Heark'ee, darling. You'll be doing me a favor if from now on you wear a round hat and have your clothes made the same way as my old sister Magdelone.

LEONORA. But, dearest, if you compare my clothes and Auntie's, you'll find hers cost more.

JERONIMUS. That's not the question, poppet. It's not the cost; but those new ideas, those headdresses, those flounces, those curls that our honest forefathers knew nothing about, that's a sinful way of dressing that causes all the world's misfortunes.

LEONORA. If I'd known it was a sin, darling, I'd have given them all up.

JERONIMUS. We don't want to believe it a sin till we are warned by a sign, and then it's too late. D'you know a calf has just been born here with a crest, curls and flounces?

LEONORA. But can you believe that's true?

JERONIMUS. Bad cess to me if it isn't true. Pernille and other decent folk here in Aebeltoft have seen the calf. Heark'ee, darling, I don't feel at all like having the Christmas party tonight.

LEONORA. Has the story about the calf frightened you?

JERONIMUS. No, not at all; it isn't the first story I've heard. But I've thought it over carefully and find that these Christmas parties and games don't do any good.

LEONORA. It's all the same to me. You know yourself how little I go out into the world. You won't find many young wives like me; I'd be quite happy if there wasn't such a thing as games or dancing. I enjoy sitting at home with my work and looking after my old man.

JERONIMUS. Of course I know that, poppet. You set an example to all the young wives in Aebeltoft. The best thing I ever did was to choose such a virtuous person as my wife.

LEONORA. I can't understand how sensible people can find any pleasure in Christmas games. They are all right for children but they ought to disgust grown-ups.

JERONIMUS. And sometimes these Christmas games have bad results.

LEONORA. Both Christmas games and other big parties, darling. I don't like them at all. If it wasn't just to please you, I'd never go out any more.

JERONIMUS. But, poppet, you mustn't cut yourself off from the world altogether; you must have some pleasure now and then. Otherwise young folk may become melancholy.

LEONORA. I'faith I'm always sad at a party and I get better when I'm alone again.

JERONIMUS. Yes, quite right, my dear, but there's reason in everything. But I'm really glad you don't want this Christmas party tonight. I'll go out for a minute and see what my sister says about it. *(To himself as he goes out.)* What a lucky man I am to have a wife like that! I can celebrate my wedding anniversary each year as a festival.

SCENE 6

(Leonora alone)

LEONORA. What bad luck Pernille has brought on us by being such a busybody! But I hope that Auntie makes him change his mind. If I'd argued with him, he would have got worse and had a hundred suspicious ideas, but now I'll play my cards so that he'll beg me himself to go to the Christmas party, and it'll look as if I'm doing it just to please him. *(Exit.)*

SCENE 7

(Jeronimus; Magdelone)

JERONIMUS. It's no use talking, sister. I won't hear of any Christmas party. It only means a lot of expense and brings undesirable results.

MAGDELONE. Oh, my dear brother, surely you're not in earnest.

JERONIMUS. Of course I'm in earnest. I've seen too many examples of such folly. I wish I had a dollar for every girl that has lost her virginity on those occasions.

MAGDELONE. But it's a good old custom.

JERONIMUS. It's an old custom, sister, but not a good one.

MAGDELONE. I've always heard that things were better in the old days than now. Why shouldn't we follow in our forefathers' footsteps? My dear brother, you should have seen the Christmas party they had at the miller's yesterday. Aren't we as good as he is?

JERONIMUS. We're just as good, but we're more sensible. Besides we can't follow the miller's example, he has more resources than we, he can eat his Christmas cakes all the year round.

MAGDELONE. I'faith I'm not saying all this for my own pleasure but for the sake of your dear children.

JERONIMUS. Yes, there we have it. Just blame the children.

MAGDELONE. But, my dear brother, what will our neighbors think of us if we have no Christmas party this year? They'll say we've lost our faith and look on us as Turks or heathens. *(She cries.)*

JERONIMUS. What silly talk! Do you change your faith because you stop being crazy?

MAGDELONE. You call it craziness, my dear Jeronimus. I know a lot of people who despised those good old customs, but they came to a bad end.

JERONIMUS. And I know a lot who despised them and did well.

MAGDELONE. Look what happened to Christopher von Bremen, who always laughed when his wife put the Epiphany lights on the table. That man was as healthy as any one of us, but just as he was fastening the suspenders on his trousers he dropped down dead.

JERONIMUS. I suppose he *never* would have died if he had been willing to burn the Epiphany lights.

MAGDELONE. Look at Jeremiah the tobacconist, who wouldn't make a difference between the Christmas evenings and other evenings by having as much as a dish of milk-porridge and lived like a heathen all through Christmastime. In his old age he had great troubles; three of his sons failed their degree examinations one after the other.

JERONIMUS. If those rascals had studied a little more they would have passed. I've known those who got *laudabilem* and yet never ate milk-porridge. D'you think a person has to eat porridge before he goes up for an examination?

MAGDELONE. Look at what happened to Hendrik Buttercup's daughters.

JERONIMUS. Yes, and look what happened to the daughters of Hendrik Daffodil, Hendrik Buttercake, Hendrik Sauerkraut. What confounded nonsense, what silly stories! Perhaps Hendrik Buttercup's daughters lost their virginity at a Christmas party. I'm crazy to go on talking like this.

MAGDELONE. Look at what happened to Christopher Oldfox.

JERONIMUS. I'faith I don't know what happened to Christopher Oldfox or Youngfox, but I do know there'll be no Christmas party this year, for besides what I've said I have other reasons. *(Exit.)*

SCENE 8

(Magdelone; Pernille)

MAGDELONE *(crying bitterly)*. Oh, what a wretched creature I am! I wish I were dead. I've lived for forty-five years, and I've never had such a poor Christmas. Why should you drudge away in this world if you never have any pleasure? All our neighbors make such a noise you can hear them all night long and we have to live as if it's always Lent. *(She continues to cry.)*

PERNILLE. Why are you crying, Madame?

MAGDELONE. Oh, Pernille, I have good reason to cry. Anyone who has such a difficult brother as mine must—

PERNILLE. I can't believe the old man has been so rash as to hit his sister.

MAGDELONE. No, it's worse than that. He won't have any Christmas party tonight.

PERNILLE. No Christmas party? *(They both cry.)*

PERNILLE. Deuce take it if I work any longer in a house like this! I'd rather go without my wages.

MAGDELONE. I tell you, Pernille, I felt as if someone had stuck a knife in my heart when I heard it. Everyone in Aebeltoft will despise our house.

PERNILLE. I was so sure we'd have a Christmas party that I'd already invited the miller's daughter.

MAGDELONE. Yes, it will be an everlasting disgrace to our whole house. The one who put the idea in Father's head should be ashamed of himself.

PERNILLE. When Arv hears about it, he won't like it any more than the others. Poor fellow, he's been practicing all morning to be a hobgoblin.

MAGDELONE. Poor fellow, he'll be quite downhearted.

PERNILLE. You'd never believe, Madame, how perfectly he can imitate a hobgoblin; you'd almost think you saw a real one.

MAGDELONE. Oh, don't talk about it any more, my heart breaks when I think of it.

PERNILLE. But would you try again to persuade the old man, Auntie?

MAGDELONE. It's no good, Pernille, even if I went down on my knees. *(They both cry.)*

SCENE 9

(Arv; Magdelone; Pernille. Arv, wrapped in a white sheet and with two horns on his head, tries to frighten the others. They continue to cry.)

ARV. Don't be afraid, Madame. Don't cry, it's me. Don't you know me now? *(Removes his disguise.)*

PERNILLE. Yes, we knew you all right. We're crying about

something else. You're not going to dress up at the Christmas games tonight.

ARV. Why?

PERNILLE. We're not having any Christmas party.

ARV. The devil take such talk! Who will stop us?

PERNILLE. The old man has got ideas in his head and has sworn—oh!—*(All three start to cry.)*

ARV. The devil split me if I'm not going to ask the old man whose servants he thinks we are, Turks or heathens!

MAGDELONE. You'll only get a good thrashing, Arv.

PERNILLE. I've just thought of something, Madame. Suppose we get the children to worry him.

MAGDELONE. If anything could help, that would.

PERNILLE. I'faith I'll go along to the school and tackle the schoolmaster.

ARV. You can promise him a hug.

PERNILLE. Shut up, you, the schoolmaster and I know each other pretty well.

ARV. It would be a poor maid who didn't know the schoolmaster. *(Exit Pernille.)*

SCENE 10

(Jeronimus; Magdelone; Arv)

JERONIMUS What's all this about?

ARV. I'm a hobgoblin, master.

JERONIMUS *(giving him a box on the ears)*. You're a hobgoblin, eh?

ARV *(falling over)*. No, master, I'm not a hobgoblin.

JERONIMUS. What does all this mean?

ARV. I only want to be a hobgoblin.

JERONIMUS *(giving him another box on the ears)*. You only want to be a hobgoblin?

ARV. No, I don't want to be a hobgoblin.

MAGDELONE. Oh, Jeronimus, it's a shame to hit the poor boy on a holiday.

JERONIMUS. Get out, you rogue, and take a book and read it, that's the best thing for you to do.

ARV *(going off in tears)*. There's no one in the whole street that's reading a single word this holiday night.

SCENE II

(Jeronimus; Magdelone)

JERONIMUS. You should have spared me that job and given him a couple of boxes on the ear before I came.

MAGDELONE. My dear brother, I don't see why our folks shouldn't have some fun as well as the others.

JERONIMUS. You ought to be a Christmas goat too. It wouldn't look bad for an old lady like you.

MAGDELONE. I don't see why we should be considered the scum of the town.

JERONIMUS. Have you seen any of the upper classes having a Christmas party?

MAGDELONE. If we follow the whims of the upper classes all we'll give people will be snuff and good wishes.

JERONIMUS. No one holds Christmas parties in Copenhagen.

MAGDELONE. Are you talking about Copenhagen? I've heard from the schoolmaster that people there don't have much faith. There's a fellow just come from Copenhagen who has no faith at all. He doesn't even believe that Doctor Martin Luther ordered us to eat goose on Martinmas eve and he even says the world is as round as an egg, which is the worst lie I've ever heard.

JERONIMUS. It's no use arguing. Let's stop talking about it. Call the schoolmaster and the children in; I want to hear if they've learned something nice for the holiday. *(Exit Magdelone.)*

JERONIMUS *(sitting at the table with a basket of toys)*. It's an art to hand out toys to children so that they are all pleased. Christopher must have this horse with the whistle inside it. What about the cart? I'll give that to Henning. Peer must have the fiddle, as I think he's going to be a musician. Else must get the cradle with the child in it; as soon as girls are old enough to talk they think about marriage and cradles. Marie, you must be satisfied with the whistle. Oh, I almost forgot little Anne; she'll have the dangling toy with the little bells on. But there they are coming along with the schoolmaster.

Scene 12

(Jeronimus; Magdelone; Leonora; Pernille; the schoolmaster with the children. The children walk on in pairs, the schoolmaster arranging the ranks with a cane in one hand and a book in the other. He places the children in a row, makes a pedantic bow and utters the following congratulatory verses.)

Misfortune's black cloud, go! Black-wingèd mist, away!
Come, Dawn! Shine, Sun! You certainly must stay.
Prosperity, pour over us just like the Nile in foam,
Besprinkle us like dew and settle in our home.
O Fortune, let thy strength flow o'er us like a brook,
Like the birds on the branch. . . .

(He repeats this and feels in his pocket.)

JERONIMUS. Can't you find a rhyme? What about . . . Our porridge we must cook?

SCHOOLMASTER. Now I have to start again from the beginning. *(He repeats his previous lines.)*

How happy we all look!
May all go well forever with Father and Mother dear,
And may their house produce a plant with every single year.
May their big cellar hold all the ale and gin they can use,
And fish and meat and butter their dainty kitchen choose.
May grain in heaps around their farm its bounty raise aloft.
As long as there's a single soul in our good old Aebeltoft.

JERONIMUS *(touching his hat)*. Thank you, Mr. Schoolmaster. That was a beautiful poem. You must have taken a lot of trouble over it.

PERNILLE. Anyone else would have had to rack his brain over it, but the schoolmaster can do anything.

JERONIMUS. But what interesting things have the children learned for the holiday? Last year they knew so many strange proverbs. Do they know any this year?

SCHOOLMASTER. Yes, will you have proverbs or riddles?

JERONIMUS. They're both good. Let Arv come in, so he can hear how the small children can show him up. *(Pernille runs for Arv, who enters and stands with his hands folded, listening.)*

JERONIMUS. Mr. Schoolmaster, first ask Arv, and then let one of the children tell him so that he's ashamed.

SCHOOLMASTER. Arv, who was it that shouted so loud that he was heard over the whole world?

ARV *(scratching his head)*. It was a . . . a hobgoblin.

JERONIMUS. He's still got that hobgoblin in his head.

SCHOOLMASTER. Christopher, Henning, Peer, Else, Marie, Anne, who was it that shouted so loud that he was heard all over the world?

ALL. A donkey in the ark, because the whole world was inside there.

JERONIMUS. Shame on you, you big rascal! The children can teach you.

SCHOOLMASTER. Arv, how far is it from here to the glass heaven?

ARV. It's fifty miles to Mariager.

SCHOOLMASTER. Christopher, Henning, Peer, Else, Marie, Anne, how far is it from here to the glass heaven?

ALL. As far as it is from the glass heaven to the crystal heaven.

JERONIMUS. Now, children, everyone point your finger at Arv. *(They all point their fingers at him.)*

SCHOOLMASTER. Arv, how many heavens are there?

ARV. There's a heaven on every bed, so there are as many heavens as beds.

SCHOOLMASTER. Christopher, Henning, Peer, Else, Marie, Anne, how many heavens are there?

ALL. There are seven heavens; one above the other.

JERONIMUS. Point your fingers at him again.

CHILDREN. Oh, oh, oh . . .

SCHOOLMASTER. Christopher, the first heaven?

CHRISTOPHER. The blue heaven.

SCHOOLMASTER. Henning, the second heaven?

HENNING. The milky heaven.

SCHOOLMASTER. Peer, the third heaven?

PEER. The glass heaven.

SCHOOLMASTER. Fold your hands nicely when you are being questioned. *(They fold their hands.)*

SCHOOLMASTER. Else, the fourth heaven?

ELSE. The crystal heaven.

SCHOOLMASTER. Marie, the fifth heaven?

MARIE. The diamond heaven.

SCHOOLMASTER. Anne, the sixth heaven?

ANNE. The pearly heaven.

JERONIMUS. There's still one left.

SCHOOLMASTER. Arv, the seventh heaven?

ARV. It's the one next to the eighth.

JERONIMUS. He's a regular idiot. He never looks at a book the whole year round and so he doesn't know any more than a Turk or a heathen. Can they answer any more questions, Mr. Schoolmaster?

SCHOOLMASTER. Yes. Arv, what is as round as an egg and as long as a church wall?

ARV *(aside)*. The devil split him and his questions. *(Aloud.)* It's a pipe; the head is round and the tail is long.

SCHOOLMASTER. Christopher, Henning, Peer, Else, Marie, Anne, what is as round as an egg and as long as a church wall?

All. A ball of thread. When you unwind it, it's as long as a church wall.

Jeronimus. Point your fingers at Arv again, children.

Children. Oh, oh, oh . . .

Jeronimus. Thank you, Mr. Schoolmaster, on behalf of my children. I see you work hard with them; you'll get a nice New Year's present. *(Jeronimus hands out the toys to the children.)* Now go into the nursery and behave yourselves nicely. I had thought of having a Christmas party, but for various reasons I've changed my mind. *(The children cry.)* Well, it can't be helped, children. I won't have such craziness in my house any more; I'm against it, and your mother is even more so. *(He turns his back to them.)*

Pernille. Go and torment him. *(The children hang on to him and shout for a Christmas party.)*

Jeronimus. That's enough, children. You've got your toys to play with. *(The children hold him tight and shout again for a Christmas party.)*

Jeronimus. Just ask your teacher if it's any use. What do you say, Mr. Schoolmaster?

Schoolmaster. Pliny, a wise and clever Roman nobleman, talks very elegantly about games and sports as follows: *Anima fulturis corporis nititur*, and in another place: *Graves seriosque mores lusibus jocisque distinguere identidem soleo.* That means: At times for the sake of my bodily health I set aside my serious habits and modesty and go in for childish games.

Pernille. That man spoke like an angel.

Schoolmaster. Now if a modest gentleman in Rome found this necessary and decent, how much more necessary and decent it is for us in Aebeltoft. I myself will add this: that as hobgoblins and subterranean folk spoil the big festivals with their weeping and wailing because they have no share in them, then we should be happy and enjoy ourselves so as to show that we do take part in them. For just as the phoenix, that lives in Arabia, lives a thousand years alone and sets fire to himself as soon as he produces his offspring, because he will not live together with others of his kind, so we human beings, on the other hand, should get together and have fun so as to show we are not related to such a brute beast. *Anthropos*, says Aristotle, *esti zoon politikon, id est: homo est animal sociabile*, and so, just as the bird of paradise—

JERONIMUS. That's enough, Mr. Schoolmaster. I see I must give in. That comparison with the phoenix was so striking. I agree that we should have a Christmas party. Now, little ones, enjoy yourselves and thank your teacher for the party. *(The children jump and shout for joy.)*

JERONIMUS *(to Leonora)*. Darling, I know you don't care much for parties. If you don't want it, I'll stick to my first decision.

LEONORA. To tell you the truth, I'd rather not have it, but as we've already invited our neighbors, I'll put up with it because of that.

PERNILLE. Oh, that nice phoenix! The other birds are just no good in comparison.

JERONIMUS. Get ready and bring in the Epiphany lights.

LEONORA. All right, it's about time; we'll have the neighbors here before we know it. *(Everything is arranged, and Arv enters and places the Epiphany lights on the table.)*

SCENE 13

(The characters in the previous scene; some visitors. The visitors enter one after the other and pay their compliments. Some of them are disguised in strange costumes. Finally Leander's landlord and landlady enter, with Leander, who is well dressed.)

LANDLORD. We hope that you, Mr. Jeronimus, and Madame will not mind us bringing a good friend of ours along. He's like a brother in the house and is a stranger here, so we want him to have a little fun.

JERONIMUS. He's very welcome.

LEANDER. Monsieur and Madame, I ask most humbly that you forgive my boldness. My landlord and landlady assured me that you, Mr. Jeronimus, were much too kind to take any offense. I'm a stranger in this place and have no pleasures except what these good people arrange for me. *(As he pays these compliments Leonora turns her back to him.)*

JERONIMUS. Don't turn your back to the visitor. My poor wife is very shy with strange men.

LEANDER. Fair lady, I think you are lucky to have such a reasonable husband who, so far from being suspicious because of your beauty, takes pleasure in seeing you associate with young men.

JERONIMUS. Just this once, Monsieur, just this once.

LEANDER. For, beautiful Leonora—

JERONIMUS. That word "beautiful" is not suitable for my wife, Monsieur; she doesn't pretend to be beautiful. It's enough for her to please me.

LEANDER. For, I say, if—

JERONIMUS. That's enough. We're simple folk, Monsieur, and don't understand compliments. Please sit down here by my sister.

LEONORA. Darling, I can't stand that man.

JERONIMUS. It doesn't matter; you must be polite.

LEONORA. No one asked him to come here.

JERONIMUS. But we must treat him politely because of our neighbors, as he is lodging in their house.

LEONORA. I hate these young whippersnappers like the plague. Did you notice how offended he was when you took him away from me and asked him to sit with old Auntie?

JERONIMUS. I should be sorry to cause him any displeasure.

LEONORA. The more displeased he is the happier I am.

JERONIMUS. No, that's no way to talk. We must show him we know how to live. Now I want you to sit together, to show him he's welcome.

Leonora. Darling husband, please don't make me sit by him.

Jeronimus. Now, do me that favor. I have my reasons.

Leonora. But, dear husband, I'll be in a bad humor all evening.

Jeronimus. Well, if it's going to put you in a bad humor, poppet, I'll not persuade you.

Leonora. Very well, for the sake of his landlord and landlady I'll sit by him, but it's against my will.

Jeronimus. That's right, poppet. That's the proper thing to do. *(She sits down next to Leander.)*

Jeronimus *(aside)*. I don't believe there's another wife like her in the whole town. The poor woman's sitting as if she has armor on and is doing it all for my sake. Ha, ha!

(They begin the Christmas games with forfeits. The schoolmaster has to sing a song. Arv has to be polite and then rude to Jeronimus, so he pays him a compliment first face to face and then with his back turned. Pernille has to go out with a man she chooses and count the stars. She picks her partner, who leads her to the front of the stage and says:) My sweet Pernille, let's go up into the hayloft; the higher we are the better we can see the stars.

Pernille. Of course. *(They go off together. Meanwhile the games continue. Arv comes in, his face blackened; in his mouth he has a stick with two candles on it; he is riding on two men with their backs to each other. The children are afraid and begin to cry. Jeronimus tells them to be quiet, that it is only Arv. After this is over Pernille comes in again with her partner.)*

Jeronimus. You good people took a long time to count the stars.

Pernille *(rubbing her mouth)*. Yes, master, there's a heap of stars in the sky.

Leonora *(taking Jeronimus aside)*. Listen, dearest, don't let's play these forfeit games any more. It might happen that this horrid fellow who is sitting with me will have to kiss me, and that would be a pity, as it's something I could not stand at all.

JERONIMUS. I wouldn't like it either, to tell you the truth. But what shall we play?

LEONORA. Let's play blind-man's buff. It's a decent game and amusing as well.

JERONIMUS. Well, just as you like. Heark'ee, my friends, we're going to play blind-man's buff.

PERNILLE. I'faith I think it's the best game. Let me be blindfolded first. *(Leonora brings Pernille downstage and bandages her eyes.)*

PERNILLE. You're tying the bandage too tight, Madame; if I can't see anything, I won't be able to get hold of the old man, as we arranged with Leander. That's better; now I can see as much as I need. *(She goes round a little, groping, and at last gets hold of Jeronimus, who won't play until the whole company compel him to. While Jeronimus is blindfolded Leonora and Leander move downstage.)*

LEANDER. Oh, most gracious Leonora, now's the time we've had so much trouble to arrange.

LEONORA. Go out into the passage at once; I'll come out another way and meet you. *(Leander goes off at one side and Leonora a little later at another. Meanwhile Jeronimus is the blind man and Pernille arranges it so that he cannot catch anyone, for whenever he is near another person, Pernille shouts to him to turn round. In the end he gets annoyed, as it goes on so long, and loosens the bandage. He misses his wife and Leander, runs out, and comes back dragging them in.)*

JERONIMUS *(shouting)*. Oh, you chaste Lucretia! Was that why I had to play blind-man's buff? And you, Monsieur Jean de France, you'll pay for this. I'll teach you to go down on your knees to a decent man's wife. *(He seizes him by the throat. Leander's landlord and landlady catch Jeronimus by the hair. Everyone takes sides, so that the whole company get into an altercation. The children cry. Jeronimus lies on the floor calling for the police, and so do the others. The schoolmaster creeps under the table. The watch are heard whistling outside and then enter.)*

The Watch *(enter, shouting)*. Come along to the town-hall, you dogs, all of you! Is this the way to keep the Christmas season holy? Don't you know what the magistrates announced a little while ago?

Jeronimus. They're trying to murder me in my own house.

Leander's Landlord. We thought an honest man lived here, but he's a murderer.

The Watch. Quick, quick, all of you to the town-hall! Tomorrow we'll hear what it was all about. Come along, you old bandit! *(They drag them all away. The women and children follow.)*

Schoolmaster *(who has remained under the table, peeps out, finally gets up, and says to the audience)*. Please accept this Christmas party. If the confounded watch had not come, it would have lasted longer and it would not have stopped with this, but— Well, you can imagine what I mean.

Diderich the Terrible

[DIDERICH MENSCHENSKRAEK]

A COMEDY IN ONE ACT

1724

DRAMATIS PERSONÆ

LEANDER, *in love with Hyacinth*
HENRIK, *his servant*
HYACINTH, *Leander's sweetheart*
EPHRAIM, *a Jew*
JERONIMUS, *Leander's father*
ELVIRE, *Jeronimus's sister*
CAPTAIN DIDERICH MENSCHENSKRAEK ("the Terrible")
HIS WIFE
CHRISTOPHER MAURBRAEKKER ("Battering-ram"), *his servant*
A CORPORAL

DIDERICH THE TERRIBLE

Scene — Venice

SCENE I

(Leander; Henrik)

LEANDER. What's the time now, Henrik?

HENRIK. It's time we saw her at the window.

LEANDER. Oh, bad cess to that Jew!

HENRIK. You shouldn't curse your neighbor and fellow-Christian, but this morning I couldn't help cursing Ephraim.

LEANDER. He was so pitiless that he threatened to complain to my father just because I stood in the doorway and talked to the girl. He drove her in brutally and swore she'd never be allowed to go out of her room again.

HENRIK. There's no sympathy or Christian charity in those Jews. But where the devil did he get that beautiful girl?

LEANDER. She's a Venetian and her parents lived in Dalmatia. She was carried off as a prisoner in the last Turkish war and sold to this Jew by Turkish merchants.

HENRIK. But what good will it do you, sir, to talk to her? It will only make you love her and you'll get more and more restless.

LEANDER. I can't help it, Henrik. I must see if I can find out what the Jew intends to do with her, and then you must help me to get her out of his clutches.

HENRIK. You must have a deuced high opinion of me. Even if I had a dozen men's brains, like the bear, I couldn't get anywhere with that fellow. It needs more than a human brain to cheat a Jew.

LEANDER. You've a head that can figure something out and a desire to do everything for me.

HENRIK. I certainly would like to do something. I tell you, sir, that I want to cheat a Jew so much that I'd gladly do it even if I was sure I'd be hanged the next day. But there's the girl at the window.

Scene 2

(Hyacinth; Leander; Henrik)

HYACINTH. Oh, isn't that Leander I see?

LEANDER. My darling!

HYACINTH. Dearest Leander, how are you?

LEANDER. My sweet girl, I've been almost dead but I've come to life again now you are here.

HYACINTH. Oh, I fear my presence is very little comfort to you.

LEANDER. Yes, there's too great a distance between us.

HYACINTH. My tyrant of a master prevents me from going near you.

LEANDER. What is he going to do with you?

HYACINTH. My blood runs cold when I think of it. He's just told me I've been sold to an officer who saw me a few days ago.

LEANDER. Oh, that is fatal news.

HYACINTH. Yes, and what's more, Leander, he's going to take me away today.

LEANDER. Oh, heavens, what are you telling me?

HYACINTH. Oh, can you help me?

LEANDER. I can help myself but not you. I can kill myself.

HYACINTH. Oh, don't do that; think of some plan instead.

LEANDER. Henrik, you must give me some advice.

HENRIK. Where the devil would I get any advice from?

LEANDER. Help me, or you're a dead man!

HENRIK. Why the devil don't you run up to her?

LEANDER. Are you crazy? Can I fly?

HENRIK. Can I go through walls?

LEANDER *(drawing his sword)*. Quick, give me some advice, or I'll kill you straight off.

HENRIK *(on his knees)*. Oh, sir, I think the devil's really riding you. Are you going to murder me because I can't do what's impossible?

LEANDER. I don't want to hear any talk.

HYACINTH. Dear Leander, don't hurt your servant. At least give him time to think.

LEANDER. Then stand up. Will you promise to find some way out?

HENRIK. That's a bit better. But to say "I want you at once to get me a girl that is locked up" is like saying "Hit your head against the wall or blow up half a score of locks or fly to the moon, so as to help me!"

LEANDER. Oh, Henrik, I rely absolutely on you.

HENRIK. I notice that, when you draw your sword to kill me.

LEANDER. Love has made me so furious that— But will you work for me?

HYACINTH. Give him time to think, dear Leander, and go off for a while.

LEANDER. Dearest lady, let me kiss your hand before I leave you.

HENRIK. That sort of talk drives me crazy. It's like saying "Cut off your hand, darling, and throw it down into the gutter, so that I can kiss it." Even if you were on stilts, sir, you couldn't reach her hand.

LEANDER. Yes, that's true, but—

HENRIK. But if it's any help, I can lift you up onto my head.

LEANDER. Yes, see if that's any good. *(Henrik raises him up onto his head.)*

SCENE 3

(The Jew; Leander; Henrik)

JEW. Hi, police, police! *(Leander and Henrik fall down and run off.)* I'll stop this at once. But you, Miss, I tell you you're going to be unlucky. You'll see. I'd rather keep jewels in my house than a girl. She's a dangerous piece of goods. I must go at once to his father and tell him about it. He lives right here. *(He knocks on Jeronimus's door.)*

SCENE 4

(Jeronimus; the Jew)

JERONIMUS. Good day, Ephraim. Do you want to speak to me? I've nothing to exchange just now.

JEW. Nor I, Mr. Jeronimus. But I have a complaint. I'm not safe in my house; I must move away from the neighborhood.

JERONIMUS. Is somebody in the neighborhood annoying you?

JEW. Your son and your servant are trying to run off with a girl in my house.

JERONIMUS. What's this I hear? Is that true?

JEW. I caught them just now in the act. But he's going to be disappointed; today the girl is to be handed over to an officer who's paid me for her.

JERONIMUS. Oh, is it possible that my only son has fallen into such debauchery? I was glad, dear Ephraim, she was the only one in your house; I'll have no peace before I hear she's gone.

JEW. There's no danger. I'll keep her well until the soldier's servant comes to get her.

JERONIMUS. Go at once, Ephraim, and let me know how it turns out.

JEW. Goodbye for now.

JERONIMUS. Leander and Henrik! Where are you two rascals? Oh, out here.

SCENE 5

(Jeronimus; Leander; Henrik)

JERONIMUS. Oh, are you there, you two brigands? I've been hearing fine news about you.

HENRIK. What have we done wrong? We've been writing all day.

JERONIMUS. Hold your tongue, you beast! My stick will soon talk on your back.

LEANDER. Why are you so angry with us, Papa?

JERONIMUS. Oh, it's just nothing—just because you're a lewd fellow, a whoremonger, a ravisher, a brigand.

HENRIK *(aside)*. He won't be in any need when he has four such fine jobs. He can live on each of them.

LEANDER. Those are harsh names that I don't deserve.

JERONIMUS. Do you know the man who lives over there?

LEANDER. Yes, he's a Jew.

JERONIMUS. And do you know the girl who's in the house too?

LEANDER. No, i'faith I don't.

JERONIMUS. Listen to that! He dares to deny what he's just done.

HENRIK. Oh, sir, just say what it is right out. You have nothing to be ashamed of. Listen, Mr. Jeronimus, it isn't for me to correct the master, but I only want to tell you that this Jew has bought a lady of good family and my master is deeply in love with her. And I'm trying with all my might to think of some way of getting her out of the Jew's hands. That's the whole affair. It's something that anyone might know and that a father ought to be pleased about.

JERONIMUS. Bad cess to you! A father ought to be pleased about that?

HENRIK. Yes, a father ought to be glad his son's following in his footsteps. Didn't you tell me, Mr. Jeronimus, that you were quite crazy once about a lady abroad?

JERONIMUS *(raising his stick)*. You dog, do you dare to reproach me—

HENRIK. Not at all. It's to your credit, Mr. Jeronimus. I wouldn't give twopence for a young man who didn't fall in love.

JERONIMUS. There's love and love. This is a shameful love for a girl that nobody knows. I've been wild in my youth; I confess my faults; but I've regretted my sins and done penance for them.

Henrik. Monsieur Leander will do penance too when he's old.

Jeronimus. That confounded boy will drive me crazy.

Henrik. Oh, Mr. Jeronimus, let him have his fling. A young man who has had no love affairs has nothing to talk to his friends about; he has to sit like a dumb animal. I'd rather have a bad character than have people say I've never been in love.

Jeronimus. Heark'ee lad! I can tell you that both you and your master are going to be disappointed. The girl is being taken away today by an officer who has bought her, and in the meantime the Jew's not going to leave his house before she's gone. So I can take it quite easy; if there was any danger, I'd go to a lot of trouble to stop it. (*Exit.*)

Scene 6

(Henrik; Leander)

Henrik. And just because of that I'm not going to take it easy. I'm going to a lot of trouble to help.

Leander. Oh, Henrik, I can't see how we can manage it.

Henrik. If you weren't my master, I'd say you were as stupid as an oyster, but as you are my master, I can only say you are like a horse, because I know the respect a servant must show. When there's no chance of a rescue, you want to kill me unless I help you at once. But when I give you some hope, then everything's impossible.

Leander. You can tell me anything you like if only you help me. But what do you suggest?

Henrik. You wouldn't understand it even if I told you. You have nothing to do except go to our neighbor who lives next door to the Jew and ask him to let me go in and out of his house. And you must get me a Jew's dress and a soldier's uniform; I'm going to play the part of two people today. Run off at once and arrange this. We haven't any time to waste. *(Exit Leander.)*

Scene 7

(Henrik; the officer's wife)

Henrik. I must watch the soldier's servant if I'm not going to miss my two meals today. If I find he knows the Jew I'll pretend to be his brother and say he's given me power to hand over the girl. If he doesn't know him, I'll pretend to be the Jew himself. But what does this lady want here?

Lady. Oh, how unfortunate we officers' wives are! We seldom see our husbands and when they do come home, they bring their mistresses with them.

Henrik *(aside)*. Heavens, can she be the wife of the officer who is going to have the girl?

Lady. I've been told that the vile strumpet he has bought is in this Jew's house.

Henrik *(aside)*. Hurrah! I've just got a new plan.

Lady. I'll wait here till the servant comes to get her and then I'll call people to help stop it. Oh, what an unhappy woman I am!

Henrik. I must talk to her. Heark'ee, dear lady, what's the matter? You look so unhappy.

Lady. Oh, my friend, will you help me? You'll be repaid for your trouble.

Henrik. You only have to command your humble servant.

Lady. My husband is coming home from the army and I hear he has bought a harlot who is in that Jew's house and he's going to take her away today. Oh, please stay here and stop her being taken off.

Henrik. My dear lady, you've come to the right man. I'm on guard here just to help you.

Lady. I thank you from the bottom of my heart.

Henrik. There's nothing to thank me for, gracious lady; I'm helping you for my own sake, not for yours.

Lady. How's that?

Henrik. My master is deeply in love with that same girl, and as he's heard she is going to be carried off today, I'm here to stop it and play a trick on the servant.

LADY. Oh, is that possible? May I give you my humble opinion? I think it would be best to watch out till the servant comes to fetch her. Then I'll call for help, and when the chance comes, you can carry her off.

HENRIK. No, dear lady, I have other plans. The Jew is known all over the neighborhood; every second house in the street has the honor of paying him twelve per cent each year. Besides, my master's father, who has got a hint of his son's love, will help the Jew all he can, so we'd get nothing from this plan except that you would be fined, I'd be put in jail, and the Jew would get his girl back. I see you're used to fighting in the open country where you go straight to work, but here in town you must go in a roundabout way if you're to get what you want. I tell you, my dear lady, I need to think so much to bring this off that every sinew in my head is stretched like a bow.

LADY. Oh, if only it could succeed!

HENRIK. It *will* succeed. . . . But what's your husband's name?

LADY. He's called Hans Frands Diderich von Menschenskraek (the Terrible).

HENRIK. Heavens! If that name was on a stone, you could kill an English bull with it.

LADY. It surely is a fine name. My husband has a lot of fun with it just as he does with everything else.

HENRIK. Listen, lady. I hope the girl will be in my hands before evening. We'll dress you in her clothes and the servant will take you away instead of her.

LADY. Good gracious, what a splendid plan!

HENRIK. Yes, I know some good plans. If you will come inside this house, I'll tell you a little more about the arrangements.

LADY. We haven't much time; I've found out that within an hour the servant—

HENRIK. Is the servant smart?

LADY. No, he's not too clever, as you can see from this story. He was at one time the company drummer and used to go to the post office for letters, and when he saw some letters with Infantry Lieutenant, Infantry Captain, Infantry Major, he thought the word Infantry should be on all letters, so when he wrote a letter to a farmer in the country, he addressed it: Mr. Lars Erichsen, Infantry Farmer.

HENRIK. Ha, ha, ha! That's pretty good; let's go in. *(Exeunt.)*

SCENE 8

(Jeronimus; Elvire)

JERONIMUS. Isn't it a damnable business? But I see they've all gone—

ELVIRE. You're always in trouble, my dear brother. But that happens to everyone.

JERONIMUS. I can feel it coming, just as some people can feel the bad weather in their limbs before it comes. An hour before I had the honor of your visit I got a pain in my right toe, and as often as that damned pain comes, something's sure to go wrong, and that's already happened, as even if the Jew's on his guard and my son's disappointed, his wicked plan has injured me.

ELVIRE. Oh, my dear brother, you take everything too seriously. I've had more trouble than you. In one year I lost the two people who were dearest to me in the whole world—my husband, who was killed in the war, and my only daughter Leonora, who was carried off as a slave while still young.

JERONIMUS. That's true, sister. You've had plenty of trouble. But, believe me, it's sadder to have wicked children than to lose them.

ELVIRE. Don't talk like that. Can anything be more sad than to lose a husband and see your only child carried off by barbarians and your house robbed?

JERONIMUS. That's true, Elvire, but I'm angry and sad every day because of my depraved son. No matter how great your sorrow is, it can be forgotten, but I'm tormented and made angry every day. You've lost your dear husband and daughter, but you can thank God that you kept your big estate in Dalmatia and sold it at a profit, so that you can live well in Venice.

ELVIRE. I can live well but not happily. Oh, if only Heaven would favor me by letting me find out where my dear daughter is, I would use all of my money, no matter how much, to get her back.

JERONIMUS. If only that could be. I had decided, with your permission, sister, to marry her to Leander. If your misfortune had not happened, my son would not have gone in for this craziness. According to my reckoning, your daughter Leonora would now be sixteen.

ELVIRE. Did you make a note of it, brother?

JERONIMUS. Yes. Among other strange things that have happened to me I wrote down in this book the birthdays both of my own and your children. I'll tell the date straight away. *(He wets his fingers and turns over the pages.)* It must be here. I'll read the whole page. On January twenty-first between eight and nine there was a very heavy cloud in the sky, a certain sign of rain, but it passed over. On the twenty-second the air was quite misty.

ELVIRE. But, my dear brother, what's the use of writing down trifles like that?

JERONIMUS. Wait a minute, I'll soon find it. On the twenty-fourth I saw a pretty girl in the square and I persuaded her to— No, that's not what I'm looking for.

ELVIRE. Keep on reading that last bit, so that I can hear about some of your tricks and then I'll be able to argue with you when you give Leander a tongue-lashing.

JERONIMUS. Wait a bit, dear sister, I'll soon find the place. On the twenty-fourth of the same month my late lamented brother Alfonso gave me a dirty dig at a party, and I've made a note of it so as not to forget to have my revenge.

ELVIRE. That was a very Christian act.

JERONIMUS. Wait a bit, dear sister; now I'm getting to the right place. On the twenty-fourth the heel came off one of my shoes, and— No, that's not right either. On the twenty-fifth I dreamed that— It must be on one of these pages. *(He reads the page quickly, muttering as he does so.)* Here it is. On the twenty-eighth my niece Leonora was born. May she grow up decent and virtuous, a joy and satisfaction to her parents and friends. Amen! I was sure it was here. But something's missing.

ELVIRE. What's that?

JERONIMUS. There ought to be on the same page: The same date my dear son Leander was changed into a werewolf.

ELVIRE. Oh, my dear brother, don't speak so bitterly.

JERONIMUS. If that had happened, I wouldn't be annoyed every day now.

ELVIRE. It will be all right when he gets older. Let's go in. *(Exeunt.)*

SCENE 9

(Henrik, dressed as a Jew; Christopher Maurbraekker, "Battering-ram")

HENRIK. I thought I saw through the window a face decorated with mustaches. Yes, i'faith, there's the ugly devil watching these houses. If only it was him.

CHRISTOPHER. This is the street. If only I could find the house.

HENRIK *(aside)*. You'll find the house all right.

CHRISTOPHER. I've never been in this town before.

HENRIK. Then it will be all the easier to cheat you.

CHRISTOPHER. It would be a pleasure to loot a town like this.

HENRIK. And it's a pleasure to swindle a fellow like this. But I'd better tackle him straight away. Good morning, sir. I see you're a stranger. Who d'you want to talk to?

CHRISTOPHER. Is there anyone living on this street?

HENRIK. Of course. I live in the smallest house.

CHRISTOPHER. I have a letter for a man that lives in the street.

HENRIK. Is the man one of the children of Israel?

CHRISTOPHER. No, he's a Jew.

HENRIK. Well, the children of Israel *are* Jews.

CHRISTOPHER. I never knew that.

HENRIK. Are you Mr. Menschenskraek's servant?

CHRISTOPHER. Yes, of course. I believe you're the man I'm looking for.

HENRIK. My name's Ephraim.

CHRISTOPHER. I think that's it. Let me see the address: Mr. Ephraim, a deserving Jew, etc. Yes, that's all right. I was told you lived around here.

HENRIK. Yes, that's my house; but what's your name, mounseer?

CHRISTOPHER. Christopher Battering-ram. Do you want to read the letter?

HENRIK. I know what's in it. You want a girl who is in my house.

CHRISTOPHER. That's about it. And here's my master's signet as proof, besides the letter.

HENRIK. Good. Oh, Hyacinth, come out! She'll be out at once.

SCENE 10

(The officer's wife, disguised; Henrik; Christopher Maurbraekker)

HENRIK. Heark'ee, Hyacinth, you must go with this man.

CHRISTOPHER. Is she good-looking, Ephraim?

HENRIK. Of course, or else your master wouldn't have paid so much for her.

CHRISTOPHER. How much more money are you going to get?

HENRIK. He's given me twenty ducats and I'm going to get a hundred and twenty more. I've often dealt with him before without anything being signed and sealed.

CHRISTOPHER. I'll take her off to some other place till the master comes home; his wife mustn't know anything about it.

HENRIK. Is she jealous?

CHRISTOPHER. Yes, I'll tell you something if you'll keep it quiet.

HENRIK. I swear by our God Mahomet and our holy Jewish Alkoranometh.

CHRISTOPHER. Well, his wife's a donkey. I'd never mind, even if she was not as old and ugly as she is, and my master in the best years of his life. Why can't he keep a mistress like all the other officers in the regiment?

HENRIK. You're quite right.

CHRISTOPHER. But however much the old hag spies she'll still be cheated. Goodbye, Ephraim. My master will see you himself in half an hour and pay you.

HENRIK. Goodbye, Christopher Battering-ram. *(Exeunt Christopher and the officer's wife.)* This last story gives me an idea for a new trick to get the money that the Jew was going to have.

SCENE II

(Henrik; Leander)

HENRIK. Come out, master.

LEANDER. Have they taken her away?

HENRIK. Yes, the first act in the comedy is over, but the servant will get into trouble for what he said about his mistress. Heark'ee sir, you keep watch while I change my clothes. *(He goes inside.)*

LEANDER. The officer's been swindled, that's certain. If only they could help me. It begins to seem possible. I'm only afraid the Jew will recognize Henrik, but he's quick and can change his speech. The Jew has only seen him once, and his clothes will disguise him. Oh, if only it could succeed! I'm filled with fear and hope. Every moment is an eternity to me. If I don't get what I want, I can't live. I believe love never affected a person's soul as it has mine. . . . But there he is, bad cess to him! I can scarcely recognize him myself.

HENRIK. Just you go in till I'm back with the booty.

LEANDER. Good luck! *(Exit.)*

SCENE 12

(Henrik, in uniform; the Jew)

HENRIK. Now it's getting serious. I must try to be brutal, then he'll believe me. *(Bangs loudly on the door.)*

JEW *(from inside)*. What's all that noise outside my door?

HENRIK. Open up, poltroon, or I'll break the whole house down.

JEW. Who are you?

HENRIK. I'm Christopher Battering-ram.

JEW. Christopher Battering-ram! That's a strange name.

HENRIK. That name's a proud one. Open up!

JEW. A little patience, sir.

HENRIK. What d'you mean, patience? I'm an officer.

JEW. And I'm a resident citizen here.

HENRIK. That's just like saying: "You're Joergen the Hatmaker and I'm Alexander the Great." Open up, or you're a dead man!

JEW *(coming out)*. What do you want, mounseer?

HENRIK. Perhaps you don't know Christopher Battering-ram?

JEW. No, sir.

HENRIK. Haven't you read my name in the papers?

JEW. No, Mr. Battering-ram.

HENRIK. Haven't you heard of the battle of Ragusa?

JEW. No, sir.

HENRIK. You civilians are as stupid as oxen.

JEW. Everyone knows something; maybe I understand some things you don't understand.

HENRIK. What do you understand? Heark'ee, poltroon! What's a counterscarp?

JEW. I don't know.

HENRIK. What's a ravelin?

JEW. I don't know.

HENRIK. A company in square formation?

JEW. I don't understand that.

HENRIK. A Gregory regiment?

JEW. I'm not a soldier.

HENRIK. An approach of petards?

JEW. I don't know that either.

HENRIK. An escort, a battalion, a squadron, an order of battle, an order for the ramparts, a protective volley, a platoon, a bastion, a company, a dromedary, a military commissar?

JEW. Mounseer, I don't understand any military language.

HENRIK. Then you're as annoying as a brute beast.

JEW. Mounseer, why are you so angry with me?

HENRIK. Angry? If I was angry, you'd know about it. This is how we military men talk when we're in a good humor. But, by the way, I have a letter for a man in this house; he's a Turk or a Jew.

JEW. A Jew, sir. But who d'you come from?

HENRIK. I'm Mr. Menschenskraek's servant.

JEW. Isn't the Jew's name Ephraim?

HENRIK. Yes, it is.

JEW. I'm the man. *(Reads the letter.)* Yes, that's right. You are to get a young girl from me. You can get anything for money. I see too that the seal is the one my agent has described.

HENRIK. I'll tell you, Monsieur Ephraim, that I'm a bit hasty and I don't speak gently even to my master for, without praising myself, I'm the bravest man in the whole bastion, a man who can kill sixteen. That's why Mr. Menschenskraek gave me this important mission rather than anyone else.

Jew. Will you come in with me? *(They go in.)*

Scene 13

(Jeronimus; the Jew; Henrik; Hyacinth)

Jeronimus. What the devil was all that noise at the Jew's house? I don't see anyone there now. I expect my son or Henrik tried to sneak into the house and carry off the girl. But there they are coming out; damme if it's not the soldier's servant. We've won the game now. I'll stand here and watch for a while.

Jew. Christopher Battering-ram, now I've handed over the girl to you, take care, there's someone on the lookout for her.

Henrik. If it was Lucifer himself, I'm the man to defend her. What sort of person is he?

Jeronimus. Your servant, Ephraim. Congratulations!

Jew. Look, he's the father of the man I mentioned.

Henrik *(aside)*. Bad cess to you, you old dog! You've come at an inconvenient time. *(Aloud.)* Are you the father of that scoundrel?

Jew. Yes, but listen, Christopher Battering-ram.

Henrik. Are you his father, you villain?

Jew. But just listen.

Henrik. That dog must die. *(He draws his sword; Jeronimus gets behind the Jew; Henrik thrusts and shouts and in the end gets Jeronimus and the Jew onto the floor.)*

Jew. Oh, oh, what have I done wrong?

Henrik. Pardon me, Ephraim. I'm only trying to get at that old rogue—

Jew *(kneeling)*. Oh, Mounseer Christopher Battering-ram, spare my life.

Henrik. Who wants to rob my master of someone he holds as dear as his life.

JEW. Do listen, mounseer.

HENRIK. He'll learn that he mustn't joke with officers.

JEW. Oh, just one word, mounseer.

HENRIK. You ought to help me kill that dog.

JEW. Let me say just one word.

HENRIK. I'm the man to cut his head off, even if it's as thick as an English bull.

JEW. This man's on our side.

HENRIK. Isn't he the father of the one who—

JEW. Yes, but he's angry with his son about it.

HENRIK. That's different; I beg your pardon.

JERONIMUS. You can do me no greater service than to get her safely to your master. I'm afraid she may fall into the hands of my son's servant.

HENRIK. I give you my word, sir, that he'll be disappointed even if he has ten more with him.

JERONIMUS. There's a couple of ducats for you, Monsieur, if you'll be careful.

HENRIK. Your humble servant. If I can serve you at any other time, it will be a pleasure.

JERONIMUS. Goodbye, Monsieur Battering-ram. *(Hyacinth is crying. Henrik whispers something in her ear, upon which she is quiet and goes off with him.)*

SCENE 14

(Jeronimus; the Jew)

JERONIMUS. I tell you, Ephraim, I've never been beaten with greater pleasure. I hope you can say the same.

JEW. He must be the devil and that was no pleasure.

JERONIMUS. I noticed he was a decent fellow and strong too, so it won't be easy to get the plunder from him or to bribe him.

JEW. That's all right, Mr. Jeronimus, but I feel the way I feel.

JERONIMUS. But I got the worst of it.

JEW. You ought to get the worst, as you're nearest to your

son. Oh, oh, my shoulder! Devil take that Christopher Battering-ram!

JERONIMUS. Don't curse him; he's an honest fellow.

JEW. A little too honest, too honest.

JERONIMUS. Won't Henrik feel ashamed when he hears of this? But I see my sister Elvire coming back.

SCENE 15

(Elvire; Jeronimus; the Jew)

ELVIRE. Well, how did it go, brother?

JERONIMUS. Very well; my back's as tender from a beating as *Bœuf à la mode.*

ELVIRE. What, were you beaten, an old man like you?

JERONIMUS. I'faith I was.

ELVIRE. Who did it?

JERONIMUS. Christopher Battering-ram.

ELVIRE. Who the devil is Christopher Battering-ram?

JERONIMUS. And because he hit so well I gave him a couple of ducats into the bargain, both for myself and this good man.

ELVIRE. If I didn't know you were a sober man, brother, I'd think you'd taken a little too much.

JERONIMUS. I'll tell you what it is. The officer's servant has taken the girl away to his master, so that load is off my mind. When he heard I was the father of the person who was trying to get that same girl, he was almost furious with zeal and he would have nearly murdered me, so I'm not sorry that—

ELVIRE. I'm afraid, darling, they've played a trick on you. The name Battering-ram and that great zeal don't sound right to me. I'm wondering if Henrik could have disguised someone and made him pretend to be a soldier.

JEW. Oh, no, upon my soul it was the right man. I know his master's writing; look, here's a letter with something else in it.

ELVIRE. Well, my congratulations. But I've something else to say—

JERONIMUS. Please come into the house; we can talk a little more about it there. *(Exeunt.)*

SCENE 16

(Henrik, dressed as a Jew; Diderich Menschenskraek; Christopher)

HENRIK. Victory! The girl's in Leander's hands. The game is won, but the story's not finished. Now I'm going to act the part of a Jew again, so as to get the money from the officer that the Jew is to have. There's no end to the tricks I can play. This last one is just to make the comedy complete. But what a noise I hear. I'faith, there's Christopher Battering-ram and his master.

MENSCHENSKRAEK. Christoph!

CHRISTOPHER. Sir!

MENSCHENSKRAEK. Where's the house?

CHRISTOPHER. The one next to the corner.

MENSCHENSKRAEK. Is the girl in the house by the square?

CHRISTOPHER. Yes, but the Jew's standing there at the door.

MENSCHENSKRAEK. Good; I'll pay him and also ask him not to let anyone know about the deal. Your servant! I'm the man who made the arrangement with your comrade on the battlefield about the girl.

HENRIK. Very well, gracious sir.

MENSCHENSKRAEK. He said she belonged to you.

HENRIK. Yes, sir, that was Levi, my agent.

MENSCHENSKRAEK. Now I've come to pay you.

HENRIK. Good.

MENSCHENSKRAEK. I must thank you for trusting me although you don't know me.

HENRIK. Oh, sir, it's no merit to trust a rich man with a good reputation.

MENSCHENSKRAEK. But I ask you, my dear Ephraim, not to tell anyone about this deal.

HENRIK. Certainly not, sir. If I did, I'd lose all my profit on it.

SCENE 17

(The Jew; Henrik; Menschenskrack; Christopher; a corporal)

JEW. Adieu, Seigneur Jeronimus. My compliments. But what do these people want?

HENRIK *(aside)*. Isn't that the Jew? Bad cess to you! Now there's going to be trouble.

MENSCHENSKRAEK. Your agent got twenty ducats.

HENRIK. Quite right, sir.

JEW. What the devil's all this about?

MENSCHENSKRAEK. Here's the other hundred and twenty.

HENRIK. Very well, sir.

JEW. What's this bad news I'm hearing?

MENSCHENSKRAEK. It's rather a lot, but she's a pretty girl.

HENRIK. She's a lovely girl, a lovely girl.

JEW. Am I asleep or awake?

MENSCHENSKRAEK. But Ephraim, remember what you promised me, not to say anything about it.

HENRIK. You can depend on me, sir.

JEW. I'm going crazy; this is a swindle. Heark'ee, gracious sir, I'm Ephraim the Jew, who sold the girl.

HENRIK. You must be the devil. I know you well.

JEW. Am I not Ephraim? I must know myself.

MENSCHENSKRAEK. What the devil is all this?

HENRIK. He's a soldier in disguise, sir, a swindler.

MENSCHENSKRAEK. You're going to be sorry for this.

JEW. Oh, sir, don't believe him.

HENRIK. Rogues and thieves like him, who dress up in your uniform, often cause us trouble.

MENSCHENSKRAEK. That's right. Tell me, you dog, what regiment have you run away from?

JEW. As I'm an honest man, I tell you I'm Ephraim the Jew and I live in this house.

HENRIK. Ha, ha, ha! That's quite right—as true as you are an honest man; but you've got to prove that first.

JEW. Oh, sir, don't believe him. I *can* prove I'm the real Jew Ephraim. And to prove it I tell you that the girl was bought by my agent three days ago, that he got twenty ducats in my name, that the girl is called Hyacinth, and that his servant has shown me his seal according to our agreement when he got the girl.

MENSCHENSKRAEK. What the devil is this? Is this some conjuring trick by which one Ephraim has become two?

HENRIK. Oh, heavens, that swindler has found out all these things so as to cheat you, good sir, and a poor man like me. Oh, oh, what a bad egg he is!

MENSCHENSKRAEK. I can soon settle the matter. Christoph, who did you get the girl from?

CHRISTOPHER *(pointing to Henrik)*. Him.

MENSCHENSKRAEK. If you're lying, it will cost you your life.

CHRISTOPHER. If I get all the misfortunes in the world, I tell you this is Ephraim and the other a swindler.

JEW. Oh, what an unhappy man I am!

CHRISTOPHER. I think I knew him as a dragoon in Captain Fire-eater's company. Yes, burn me if it isn't the same man! Heark'ee, isn't your name Jokum Traekholdt?

JEW. I swear by Heaven and Earth I'm Ephraim the Jew.

HENRIK. That's right, what Christopher Battering-ram says. Now I remember his name's Jokum Traekholdt.

CHRISTOPHER. I knew the fellow at once. Have you the signet, Ephraim?

HENRIK. Yes, here's the signet. You can see now, sir.

MENSCHENSKRAEK. Here, corporal!

CORPORAL *(coming in)*. Sir.

MENSCHENSKRAEK. Arrest that man for me; he's a disguised soldier. *(Corporal drags the Jew out, crying "Oh, woe is me!")*

MENSCHENSKRAEK. What a devil of a fellow that was!

HENRIK. There's a lot of bad characters in this town.

MENSCHENSKRAEK. Ephraim, here's the money. I've counted it myself.

HENRIK. Thank you, honored sir. There was no hurry. Goodbye, your highness. *(He goes in.)*

SCENE 18

(Menschenskraek; Christopher; Jeronimus; Elvire)

JERONIMUS. The maid said there was another row out here, but everything seems to be quiet.

MENSCHENSKRAEK *(to Christopher)*. You mustn't say anything about the row, either to these people or others. The whole thing must be a secret.

ELVIRE. I believe I know this officer. Isn't it Mr. Menschenskraek?

MENSCHENSKRAEK. I'm sure I knew that lady in Dalmatia.

ELVIRE. Mr. Menschenskraek.

MENSCHENSKRAEK. Madame Elvire. (*They embrace.*) I had the honor of being received in your house when we were fighting at Ragusa.

ELVIRE. That's true, but the honor was mine. I've had great trouble since; my house was looted by the Turks and my people carried off as slaves.

MENSCHENSKRAEK. That couldn't have happened while I was campaigning. The Turks were so terrified of my name that they wouldn't try to take any plunder, I'd made them so sick of that business. I dare say that all by myself in battles here and there I killed twenty thousand men, and once during one month I massacred over two thousand Janissaries with my own hand. Isn't that so, Christopher Battering-ram?

CHRISTOPHER. Certainly.

MENSCHENSKRAEK. That's why the general himself gave me the name Menschenskraek ("The Terrible").

ELVIRE. Is that possible? Is that how you got your name?

MENSCHENSKRAEK. Yes, he himself did me the honor of presenting me to the Duke of Dalmatia with these words: Your Highness, here is a second Scanderberg, the scourge of the Turks.

ELVIRE. Really?

MENSCHENSKRAEK. Nothing was more pleasant to me than to meet a whole company of armed Turks all by myself. Isn't that so, Battering-ram?

CHRISTOPHER. Certainly.

MENSCHENSKRAEK. I had the Turkish vizier Mahometh Podolski by the heels, but just at that moment a bomb came and blew my hand back, so he escaped that time. But it's only a short respite. I'll never forget how he shrieked in Turkish: oh, la, la, la!

ELVIRE. What does that mean in our language?

MENSCHENSKRAEK. It means: Oh, great Mahomet, help me against this strong warrior Menschenskraek.

ELVIRE. Can those few words mean so much?

MENSCHENSKRAEK. Yes, the Turkish language is very rich.

ELVIRE. But may I be bold enough to ask why you are in this ordinary street today?

MENSCHENSKRAEK. Madame Elvire, you're an honest woman and I know you'll not betray me. A few days ago I bought a female slave in the camp of the agent of the Jew who lives here.

JERONIMUS. Good heavens! Is it you, sir, who bought this woman?

MENSCHENSKRAEK *(to Elvire)*. Can that man keep quiet too?

ELVIRE. Yes, I'll answer for him, Mr. Menschenskraek.

MENSCHENSKRAEK. Good, but I notice the maid is listening at the door; can she keep quiet too?

JERONIMUS. Oh, perfectly. You'd swear she wasn't a maid, she can be so quiet.

MENSCHENSKRAEK. Good! I had that girl taken away today by my servant Christopher Battering-ram.

ELVIRE. Can she speak Italian?

MENSCHENSKRAEK. Of course, she's an Italian girl.

ELVIRE. Oh, Mr. Menschenskraek, may I have the pleasure of talking to her? Maybe she can tell me something about my people, who were sold as slaves some years ago?

MENSCHENSKRAEK. Of course. Christoph! Bring the girl here at once. *(Exit Christopher.)*

ELVIRE. Is she far away?

MENSCHENSKRAEK. Just in the square, where she's boarding with a good friend of mine. My wife doesn't know anything about it.

JERONIMUS. I shouldn't have thought a man like you would be afraid of his wife.

MENSCHENSKRAEK. Certainly not. If I just wrinkle my forehead, everything in the house trembles and quakes.

JERONIMUS *(aside)*. I'll bring my son and Henrik out so they can see what a brave rival they have, and that will chase those ideas right out of their minds.

ELVIRE. How much did you pay for the girl?

MENSCHENSKRAEK. One hundred and forty ducats.

ELVIRE. She must be very pretty then.

MENSCHENSKRAEK. I don't think Venus was as perfect. But who are these two people?

SCENE 19

(Leander; Henrik; the characters from the previous scene)

JERONIMUS. It's only my son and his servant.

MENSCHENSKRAEK. Can they be quiet too?

JERONIMUS. Yes, I'll guarantee that. *(To Leander.)* I've brought you out to embarrass you and to show you what sort of rival you have.

MENSCHENSKRAEK. But, gentlemen, as I've told you one thing, I may as well tell you the other. A little while ago you heard a row out here. It was a damned funny business that almost lost me a hundred and twenty ducats. A swindler disguised as a Jew—But here's the girl coming along. Welcome, my darling.

Scene 20

(The officer's wife, disguised as a female slave; the rest)

ELVIRE. My heart bleeds when I see a slave girl.

MENSCHENSKRAEK. D'you call it a sin for a man who has a toothless old hag to keep a mistress?

ELVIRE. It's very usual.

MENSCHENSKRAEK. I just took the old crone for her money. But I only treat her as a housekeeper. She's as jealous as the devil; I've seen that, but it doesn't matter. Now you'll see a face that means something. Take that veil off, my sweet Hyacinth, and let me kiss you. *(Just as he is about to embrace her his wife thrusts her ancient face out and gives him a box on the ears.)*

MENSCHENSKRAEK. Oh, oh, oh, what's this? *(He falls to his knees. His wife hits him with a whip.)*

MENSCHENSKRAEK. Oh, oh, my darling wife, don't kill me.

JERONIMUS. Oh, Mr. Menschenskraek, is it possible that—

MENSCHENSKRAEK. Oh—oh—oh! *(His wife keeps on beating him.)*

ELVIRE. Oh, Mr. Menschenskraek, what's happening?

MENSCHENSKRAEK. Oh—oh—oh! *(His wife continues to beat him.)*

JERONIMUS. Where's that bravery of yours, Mr. Menschenskraek?

ELVIRE. Has all his manhood gone at once?

JERONIMUS. Remember the battle of Ragusa, Mr. Scanderberg.

ELVIRE. Remember the great vizier, Mr. Scourge of the Turks.

MENSCHENSKRAEK. Oh, my darling, I'll never do it again.

JERONIMUS. Christopher Battering-ram, won't you help your master?

CHRISTOPHER. No, Monsieur, my courage has gone to the devil. I'm no fighter, except on the battlefield.

JERONIMUS. You mustn't beat your husband any more, lady. *(They separate the two.)*

ELVIRE. But what on earth is all this about?

CHRISTOPHER. Somebody's played a devil of a trick on us; I believe the man we thought a swindler was the real one. I'll run after him at once. *(The officer's wife wants to beat her husband again, but the others prevent her.)*

JERONIMUS. This is terrible.

ELVIRE. It's a great piece of female cunning.

JERONIMUS. How did it happen?

MENSCHENSKRAEK. Oh, please hold my wife. Oh, oh! I don't know. The Jew who lives in this house must have made it up with my wife.

JERONIMUS. There's never been any Jew living in this house.

MENSCHENSKRAEK. Oh, oh, so the one I thought was Ephraim was a swindler.

ELVIRE. Have you been dealing with two Jews?

MENSCHENSKRAEK. There were two, and each said he was the right one. Oh, oh, what a miserable fellow I am! . . . But there's the other Jew.

SCENE 21

(The Jew; Christopher; the others; Hyacinth, later)

JEW. Oh, woe is me! Oh, woe is me! What a swindle! What a swindle!

HENRIK. Now put a bold face on it, Henrik.

JERONIMUS. Look, here's the real Ephraim. What's happened, Ephraim?

JEW. Oh, I don't know, Seigneur.

WIFE. Well, I'll tell you the whole story. I came here to stop what I'd discovered was going to happen, and I found a servant ready to help me. He took me in this house, put on Jewish clothes to cheat Christopher, gave me a slave's dress, and took me off instead of the wench. He's an honest fellow— But there's the servant standing right here.

HENRIK *(aside)*. Bad cess to you, you ugly old hag!

JERONIMUS. Good heavens, has this dog—

JEW. Yes, now I recognize his face. He took the girl.

HENRIK *(kneeling)*. Oh, Mr. Jeronimus, don't be angry with me.

JERONIMUS. You'll be beaten and put in jail. Where's the wench?

LEANDER. She's in my possession and I'll never let her go. Besides I can tell you, Father, she's no wench but a girl of good family. Her father was a rich man, and when he was away she was carried off as a slave—four years ago.

ELVIRE. What was her father's name?

LEANDER. He was called Pandolfus and he was killed in the war. I don't know whether darling Auntie could be her mother: she was called Elvire—

ELVIRE. Oh, heavens! What news! It's my daughter.

HENRIK *(getting up)*. The devil she is.

JERONIMUS. What? Is she your daughter, Elvire?

ELVIRE. Yes, let me hold her in my arms.

LEANDER. Bring her here at once, Henrik. *(Henrik runs out and comes back with the girl.)*

ELVIRE. Do you know me, daughter?

HYACINTH. Oh, my dear mother! Where did you come from? *(They embrace.)*

JEW. This is all very well, but I must have my money.

MENSCHENSKRAEK. The devil take your money! He must give it back to me.

HENRIK. I earned the money honestly.

WIFE. That's right; just keep the money.

MENSCHENSKRAEK. But, my dear wife, the money was mine.

JEW. But the goods were mine.

WIFE *(hitting them both)*. There's something for your

money, and for your goods. *(Menschenskraek cries and runs away.)*

JEW *(shouting as he runs off)*. Oh, woe is me!

ELVIRE. Let them fight it out. We'll go in and be happy together and finish this story with a proper wedding.

The Peasant in Pawn

[DEN PANTSATTE BONDEDRENG]

(A THREE-ACT COMEDY IN ONE ACT)

1726

DRAMATIS PERSONÆ

LEERBEUTEL, *a countryman who is in debt*
PERNILLE, *his maid*
PEER NIELSEN, *a peasant boy, who pretends to be a count*
LEANDER, *citizen*
JACOB, *the landlord*
THREE TOWN COUNCILORS
MADAME STAABI
A JEWELER
NIELS PERSEN } *Peer Nielsen's Parents*
GERTRUDE } *Peer Nielsen's Parents*
A POSTMAN
THE LANDLORD'S SERVANTS
ANOTHER LANDLORD
A MUSICIAN

THE PEASANT IN PAWN

Scene I

(Pernille; Leander; later, a postman)

Leander *(meeting Pernille)*. There's another eleventh of June face. Isn't it Miss Pernille? Yes, i'faith it is. Welcome home!

Pernille. I thank you most humbly, sir.

Leander. Is your mistress with you?

Pernille. No, I came just with the master.

Leander. I'faith that's strange. Your mistress can't be very suspicious when she sends the chambermaid to town with the master.

Pernille. I can tell you we've other things besides jealousy to think of these days.

Leander. What do you mean?

Pernille. That's a funny question. I suppose you haven't an almanac, sir.

Leander. Yes, of course I have.

Pernille. Then you know, sir, it's the eleventh of June today.

Leander. Why is he afraid of the eleventh of June?

Pernille. He isn't so much afraid of the eleventh of June, but the eleventh of June is dangerous for him. There's a lot of unreasonable folk in this town. Just think, Monsieur Leander! The master has been in town a week and has not been able to get a loan of the miserable ten thousand rix-dollars he needs. He has asked five or six merchants in the street we live in, but—

Leander. What's the name of the street?

Pernille. It's Vimmelskaftet. It's such a crooked street.

Leander. It will be still more crooked by the eighteenth of June.

Postman *(entering)*. Excuse me, my good friends, I believe

there's a very important man from the country lodging here.

PERNILLE. What's his name?

POSTMAN. Mr. Leerbeutel.

PERNILLE. I know him.

POSTMAN. He must be an important bankrupt.

PERNILLE. Not yet, son, but he may be. Nothing's impossible. Will you give me the letter? I'm his servant. *(The postman gives her the letter and goes off.)* But look, there he is.

LEANDER. I don't want to talk to him yet. I must go.

SCENE 2

(Leerbeutel; Pernille)

LEERBEUTEL. I can manage everyone but those damned creditors.

PERNILLE *(aside)*. Just like me.

LEERBEUTEL. They're uncivilized.

PERNILLE *(aside)*. Just louts.

LEERBEUTEL. I'd rather go around with blacksmiths.

PERNILLE *(aside)*. Or tinkers.

LEERBEUTEL. They've no respect for people of good birth and social position.

PERNILLE *(aside)*. They just treat everyone alike.

LEERBEUTEL. Hallo, is that you, Pernille? What are you doing here?

PERNILLE. I'm wondering how I could shuffle the eleventh of June out of the calendar.

LEERBEUTEL. And I'm wondering how I could shuffle myself out of the country. I get one damned letter after another.

PERNILLE. Haven't you got any money yet, sir?

LEERBEUTEL. No, Pernille. The people in this town are shameless. I've been good enough to offer certain men forty per cent, but still they won't lend me anything.

PERNILLE. That's a scandal.

LEERBEUTEL. And I've offered to pay them the interest in advance too.

PERNILLE. What mean idiots they are! All they could lose in that way would be sixty per cent. Here's a letter for you, sir.

LEERBEUTEL. Who gave you that?

PERNILLE. A prophet.

LEERBEUTEL. How d'you know he was a prophet?

PERNILLE. Well, he said the letter was for a bankrupt.

LEERBEUTEL. Perhaps he said that out of spite.

PERNILLE. No, I think he meant a banker. Will you read it, sir? *(He reads the letter.)*

LEERBEUTEL. "At three weeks sight Mr. Leerbeutel shall pay this promissory note for ten rix-dollars." You see what people think of me. Three weeks sight for ten dollars! Pernille, you've played plenty of tricks to rescue me before. Now I need your help more than ever.

PERNILLE. We'll play tricks till we're hanged in the end.

LEERBEUTEL. Oh, no, they don't hang women.

PERNILLE. I'll be glad to help you, sir, but it'll be difficult unless we do something crooked.

LEERBEUTEL. If you can't manage honestly, you have to try other ways.

PERNILLE. I can't think of anything straight off except that you go bankrupt again.

LEERBEUTEL. That might be all right if I had any money for traveling.

PERNILLE. I know you have plenty of credit, sir.

LEERBEUTEL. You can see how much credit I have from this note for ten dollars, at three weeks sight.

PERNILLE. Maybe I could find some way out if I hadn't so much conscience.

LEERBEUTEL. That's the trouble. But why don't you just leave your conscience at home?

PERNILLE. Oh, sir, it costs nothing to take around. The freight is very small.

LEERBEUTEL. Yes, I know that. It'd take a lot of consciences like yours for the mail-coach to make its expenses.

PERNILLE. That's true, it's not very heavy. But however small it is, it's still something.

LEERBEUTEL. It's very unreasonable to bring a conscience to town around the eleventh of June. But let's stop joking and think of some way out of my difficulties.

PERNILLE. Are you willing to do something crooked, sir?

LEERBEUTEL. What a funny question! I've done it so often when there was no need, and now I'm to think it over when I'm faced with so many misfortunes.

PERNILLE. I'll see if I can think of something next week.

LEERBEUTEL. To offer me help next week is like offering help in a couple of hours time to someone who has fallen in the sea.

PERNILLE. The trouble is, sir, that you have too high ideas about me. You rely too much on me.

LEERBEUTEL. I know what you can do.

PERNILLE. Yes, and I know it myself too.

SCENE 3

(Peer, a peasant boy, enters with his mouth open; Leerbeutel; Pernille)

PERNILLE. Look at that country lad standing there with his mouth open. I suppose he's never been in a market town before.

LEERBEUTEL. Heark'ee, country fellow, where's your home?

PEASANT. In a village out in the country.

LEERBEUTEL. What's the village called?

PEASANT. I'faith I don't know.

LEERBEUTEL. How far is it from here?

PEASANT. D'you mean this town here?

LEERBEUTEL. What a damned crazy fellow! Would I ask how far this town is from itself? But don't you know the name of the village you live in? What's the sheriff called? If I hear his name, maybe I can tell you the name of the village.

PEASANT. Our sheriff? Let me see . . . he has the same name as me.

LEERBEUTEL. And what's your name?

PEASANT. I'faith I can't remember. Let's see— Wait a bit, my mother would know it.

LEERBEUTEL. He's an arrant fool.

PEASANT. But I know the name of our parson.

LEERBEUTEL. What is it?

PEASANT. He's called Pastor, i'faith he is.

LEERBEUTEL. He's worse than a brute beast.

PEASANT. If you won't be mad at me, kind sir, I'd like to ask what sort of house that big house is.

LEERBEUTEL. That's the town hall.

PEASANT. Good gracious! You could put a whole lot of cows in there and feed a terrible pile of horses and bullocks there, too. I suppose you get to the stables through that big door.

LEERBEUTEL. I didn't think there could be such people. But heark'ee, my friend, what are you doing in town today?

PEASANT. Not very much. But, kind sir, don't be angry with me for asking so many questions. How do all these folks manage in town? I don't see any fields or meadows, or horses or bullocks, not even a pig.

PERNILLE. There are plenty of bulls and pigs. But the people here live on you and other peasants' sweat and work.

PEASANT. But why are we so crazy that we work for them?

PERNILLE *(to Leerbeutel)*. I'll use this fellow's stupidity, sir, and start something that will get us some money. *(To the peasant.)* You are right, old fellow, when you say you're crazy to work and sweat for others. I'm sure no one has thanked you for it since you got to town.

PEASANT. They weren't even decent enough to lift their hats when I took my cap off.

PERNILLE. Heark'ee, old chap. Would you like to stay here in town? You'll have no work to do except eating and drinking.

PEASANT. Thank you. That would be a fine life.

PERNILLE. You'll get five or six dishes at every meal.

PEASANT. Do folks get as many dishes as that in town?

PERNILLE. Certainly, most of them.

PEASANT. Then they must have bellies as big as mares.

PERNILLE. No, they only eat a little of each dish. But if you do what I tell you, you'll have the same good old time.

PEASANT. I sure will.

PERNILLE. Let's see now if you can remember everything I tell you.

PEASANT. I'll keep it in my head.

PERNILLE. Oh, I'm going crazy. It's all right for him to be an idiot, but I'm afraid he'll go too far. Heark'ee, old fellow, you must keep quite silent, and if anyone speaks to you, you mustn't answer anything but this: "Ask my steward." *You* must act the part of the steward, sir.

LEERBEUTEL. What will the country boy be?

PERNILLE. I'll make him a count. We'll pretend he's traveling abroad, and I'll be the countess. Take your coat off, sir. I must see how he looks in it. *(They put Leerbeutel's coat on him.)*

PEASANT. Eh, that's a fine coat. The lord of the manor didn't have a better coat the day he was spliced.

PERNILLE. Don't talk any more about the lord of the manor; you're a lord yourself now, a count.

PEASANT. The devil I am.

PERNILLE. Now just act as if you are our lord.

PEASANT. Is a count the same as Our Lord?

PERNILLE. No, no, just imagine I'm your wife and he's your servant, and when anyone asks you anything, you answer what I just told you. Now I'll pretend to be a stranger you have to speak to: "Your humble servant, I'm so glad to see that your grace has arrived safely." Look a little lively! "May I take the liberty of asking your grace when you got here?" Look lively! What are you going to answer?

PEASANT. What do I answer? You're acting like a fool.

PERNILLE. Well, you'll have to get used to this foolishness if you want to be a big man.

PEASANT. What should I answer?

PERNILLE. Have you forgotten so quickly? You must answer: "Ask my steward." Oh, look a little lively. Now I'll talk to you again: "When did your grace arrive in town?"

PEASANT. Ask my steward, or talk to my steward, look a little lively.

PERNILLE. Oh, bad cess to you, you stupid oaf!

PEASANT. Ask my steward— What was the other thing?

PERNILLE. Oh, you're driving me crazy. That's enough; just stop there. Now I'll say a little more: "I suppose your grace is not married yet."

PEASANT. Ask my steward.

PERNILLE. That's question's no good. I suppose your grace has come here to see our little town.

PEASANT. Look lively.

PERNILLE. Oh, I'll never get anywhere with him. He's as dumb as a mule. Don't say anything but "Ask my steward."

PEASANT. Yes, now I understand. Ask my steward.

PERNILLE. All right. There's a man living in that big house where we're going to play our comedy. You, sir, must go ahead and reserve the finest rooms for a rich count and his wife. *(The peasant blows his nose and wipes his fingers on his coat.)*

LEERBEUTEL. Shame on you! Do you wipe your fingers on my coat?

PEASANT. Ask my steward.

PERNILLE. Oh, that doesn't matter, sir. Let him have his whims.

LEERBEUTEL. I'm beginning to see what you're planning with this plot, but I'm afraid we'll be recognized.

PERNILLE. No one will recognize us with the show we'll put on. Besides, you must risk something to get out of great trouble.

LEERBEUTEL. That's true. If I don't get money somehow, I'm in a fix.

PERNILLE. And you're not risking anything, sir, it's only me.

LEERBEUTEL. That's right, Pernille. I owe you both my life and well-being. But what are we going to do first?

PERNILLE. You must go into that big inn and order the best rooms for a foreign count. You must swagger and talk big.

LEERBEUTEL. That's easy. I'm used to that.

PERNILLE. Look here, my friend, give the gentleman his coat back again.

PEASANT *(crying)*. Oh, let me keep it.

PERNILLE. You'll get it back soon. Come along with me now.

SCENE 4

(Leerbeutel; a landlord)

LEERBEUTEL. She's a fine girl and she'll go far. I must get started at once. *(He knocks at the inn-door.)*

LANDLORD. Who d'you want to talk to, sir?

LEERBEUTEL. I'm the count's steward.

LANDLORD. Which count?

LEERBEUTEL. A foreign count who's just come to town and would like to stay here as they say your inn is the best.

LANDLORD. Yes, I'm sure his grace wouldn't be accommodated better anywhere else.

LEERBEUTEL. You must see that you get us some good fish; the count doesn't care much for meat. What sort of wines have you?

LANDLORD. All kinds. I've just got some Burgundy in that's not to be scorned. But is the count far away?

LEERBEUTEL. No, he's on his way from the post-house where the carriages are being kept. He'll take a sedan chair there, as he can't bear driving over the paving-stones.

LANDLORD. Good gracious, is he coming so quickly? Henrik, get everything ready in the big hall. We're expecting guests.

LEERBEUTEL. You must hurry as fast as you can.

LANDLORD. Everything will be ready in half an hour. I hope his grace will be satisfied. Would you like me to send some of my servants to carry his baggage?

LEERBEUTEL. Oh, no, we have plenty of our own people. He has his wife with him too.

LANDLORD. Will your worship forgive me if I ask one thing? How is it that a gentleman who is already married keeps a steward?

LEERBEUTEL. My master married very young. Besides, there's another reason I'll tell you about later. Just go in now and get everything ready. My master'll be here in half an hour.

SCENE 5

(Leerbeutel; Pernille)

LEERBEUTEL. Well, that's the beginning; how it will turn out I don't know. Other people use tricky men servants to do crooked things but I use maids. But sex has nothing to do with it. It's the one with the best head and most daring that's most useful. That girl has saved me from a lot of troubles, so I feel quite hopeful that she'll succeed. As it is, I'm not risking very much, for if I fall into the hands of my merciless creditors— But there she is again.

PERNILLE. Well, sir, have you done your business?

LEERBEUTEL. The rooms are ordered and everything will be ready in half an hour. How it will work out—

PERNILLE. Just you leave it to me. I've already got hold of a lot of kind people who'll help us.

LEERBEUTEL. But where's the count?

PERNILLE. He's at my aunt's and I've told her the whole thing. Although I shouldn't praise my own relatives, she's a clever woman and so helpful that she's often risked going to jail for helping folks who pay her for her trouble.

Leerbeutel. But I'm afraid about that peasant; he's really too stupid.

Pernille. If he was half an ounce less stupid he'd be no use to me. If you only play your part as a steward as well as I act the part of the wife, we'll be all right. Let's go off now and get ready.

Scene 6

(The Count in a sedan chair, the others walking by his side; the landlord, very officious, helping him out of the chair, hat in hand)

Leerbeutel. Hey, Christopher, Peiter! Run off at once to the post-house and fetch the gentleman's baggage and trunks. The countess is coming in at the back gate.

Lackeys. Very good, Mr. Steward.

Landlord. Heaven help me, your worship, I'm afraid we haven't everything in the house we ought to have. If I had only known a little earlier about his grace's arrival, it would have been better.

Leerbeutel. I know, but I'm sure you have some rooms tidy.

Landlord. Yes, the big hall you were shown into is ready. The morning-rooms will soon be put right.

Leerbeutel. Good.

Landlord. Oh, Mr. Steward, the count seems so gracious. He's very young.

Leerbeutel. Yes, he's only eighteen and also very simple for such a great lord, so I have to do everything. What's the name of the most important broker in town?

Landlord. Andreas Grobsmidt.

Leerbeutel *(taking a paper from his pocket)*. Yes, that's the one. This letter says Andreas Grobsmidt. Can that fellow count me out four thousand rix-dollars at three days sight?

Landlord. Yes, your worship. It wouldn't matter if it was

ten thousand. But can the count need so much money all at once?

LEERBEUTEL. Certainly. A thousand dollars doesn't mean anything more to him than twopence. You could do with people like that every day, Mr. Landlord.

LANDLORD. I'faith you're right, sir.

SCENE 7

(Herman, another landlord, enters; the same characters as before)

SECOND LANDLORD. Oh, sir, I want to recommend my humble house to you; you'll be much better served than here.

FIRST LANDLORD. I'd be sorry if there was better accommodation anywhere than in my house.

SECOND LANDLORD. Oh, that makes me laugh. Why, you can't even make a decent stew, Jacob.

FIRST LANDLORD. I suppose I'd learn it from you, Mr. Herman.

SECOND LANDLORD. I know what the people said who stayed here last week.

FIRST LANDLORD. What did they say?

SECOND LANDLORD. They said they got poor accommodation and were properly swindled.

LEERBEUTEL. Now, lads, don't start a quarrel.

SECOND LANDLORD. I'm telling the truth, sir. If you come and stay with me, you'll get much better service and you'll be cheated far less than here.

LEERBEUTEL. It's too late, old fellow.

FIRST LANDLORD. Those who say I cheat people are rogues.

SECOND LANDLORD. And I say you're a dishonest fellow who is trying to take the bread out of decent folks' mouth.

FIRST LANDLORD. *You're* a dishonest fellow. *(They seize each other by the hair, and the steward separates them and drives the second landlord off.)*

Landlord. Oh, gracious Mr. Steward, don't be angry at this happening in your presence. I can't control myself, Mr. Steward, when someone attacks my good name and reputation and says I can't cook a stew. Wouldn't that hurt you, Mr. Steward? I'd rather he called me a rogue and a cheat. *(Cries.)*

Leerbeutel. Oh, Mr. Landlord, if you took everything people said to heart, you'd have enough to do. How old are you now and how long have you been cooking for people?

Landlord. Over thirty years.

Leerbeutel. In all that time I think your hot blood should have boiled off. If I'd let myself be affected by talk, I'd have been eaten up by anger long ago. In every letter I get from home there's something new from my friends, who tell me what folks are saying about our journey abroad—that I am taking advantage of the count's simplicity and using his money for myself, when I can swear that I've put over three thousand of my own money into this trip, as the countess can tell you. But, Mr. Landlord, when you have a good conscience, you can despise all that.

Landlord. If only all decent young men were in such good hands as yours! There's something strange about me, Mr. Steward; as soon as I see a person, I can say at once what sort of stuff he's made of. I'd hardly looked at you before I noticed what a sensible and good man you were. But, Mr. Steward, is the count so simple?

Leerbeutel. Mr. Landlord, one shouldn't speak ill of such great gentlemen. I'm not speaking badly of him either, for what can he do if nature has made him that way? But I can tell you—only don't repeat this.

Landlord. I'll keep my mouth shut, Mr. Steward.

Leerbeutel. I can tell you that he's scarcely human except for his appearance, and no matter how I try to hide his foolishness, observant people notice it at once. His father, the old count, has often wrung his hands, even cried about it, to me. I comfort him by saying that many as simple as he in their young days have grown sensible when they got older. His father thought that when he went abroad, he would change and become more polished, but I haven't seen any change yet. I must go up to the master now. He's invited the leading citizens to dine with him here this evening. See that we get good service, Mr. Landlord. You'll be well paid. Goodbye for now.

Scene 8

(The landlord; Madame Staabi; Leerbeutel enters later)

Landlord. That steward's a nice man. But I wish he and the lady were not here; then I could look after the count myself. We don't often get such a windfall, and we have to use the chance. An inn is like a lottery. There are a lot of blanks and small prizes, but this count is like one of the big lots in the fifth class that have to make up for the others. But look who's here. Good morning, Madame Staabi. D'you want to speak to me?

Madame Staabi. I heard that a foreign gentleman had come here. I have brocade, silk goods, and other things.

Landlord. I must wait till the steward comes back; everything goes through his hands. But here he is. Mr. Steward, here's a woman with fancy goods, if the count would like to have any.

Leerbeutel. Maybe we should have about thirty yards of brocade, but it must be good.

Madame Staabi. No one in town has better brocade, but it's rather dear. If you want good things, you've got to pay for them.

Leerbeutel. They're not really dear if they're good.

Madame Staabi. Look here, sir. If you can find patterns like this and such thick brocade in the whole town, I'll give you this for nothing.

Leerbeutel. Have you any nice snuff-boxes?

Madame Staabi. Yes; here's a gold box with a nice picture

on it, but it's worth two hundred dollars; it's made of pure ducat gold.

LEERBEUTEL. Yes, it's a nice box. I expect the count will have it and the brocade as well when he has time to look at them. Will you leave it here till tomorrow?

MADAME STAABI. Yes, certainly.

LEERBEUTEL. You can come here tomorrow at nine o'clock.

MADAME STAABI. All right.

LEERBEUTEL. But you must give me the best price on the brocade.

MADAME STAABI. Oh, we'll arrange that all right.

LEERBEUTEL. Have you any nice jewels?

MADAME STAABI. No, sir, but there's a man living just near here that I'd recommend.

LEERBEUTEL. Well, let him come along at once. *(Exit Madame Staabi.)* Mr. Landlord, the guests will soon be here. See that you treat them well.

LANDLORD. They'll be treated like kings. *(Exit landlord.)*

SCENE 9

LEERBEUTEL *(alone)*. The comedy's starting all right. Maybe it's a little rash to invite important guests who may see through us and realize at once he's a coarse peasant lad, but my teacher Pernille says the more we cut a big figure the better impression we'll make and so remove any suspicions from our host's mind. I'll certainly fool the gentlemen and she will do the same to the ladies. But there's the jeweler. These folks rush into trouble as if they were afraid they couldn't be cheated soon enough.

SCENE 10

(Leerbeutel; the jeweler)

JEWELER. Your servant, sir. Madame Staabi sent me here. I'm a jeweler.

LEERBEUTEL. Let me see what this is like. I like these best. The count may want to keep them, but he has no time to look at them now, as we are expecting some of the town councilors. If you leave them till tomorrow, you'll have an answer.

JEWELER. I'll bring the jewels again tomorrow.

LEERBEUTEL. No, sir, I'll give you some better advice. You'd better stay away as you're so afraid. There was another jeweler here just now with good recommendations and he offered to let us keep as many as we wished, but I let him go because Madame Staabi had talked to me about you.

JEWELER. Oh, my dear Mr. Steward, I didn't mean anything like that.

LEERBEUTEL. No, sir. I'd never tempt you or anyone else. You might lie awake all night thinking that you had left a couple of jewels with a count of the Holy Roman Empire.

JEWELER. Oh, don't be angry, your worship.

LEERBEUTEL. I'm not at all angry. I admire your caution.

JEWELER. Oh, your worship!

LEERBEUTEL. I tell you, sir, I'm not offended in the least, but you can't hold it against me if I deal with whoever I like.

JEWELER. Oh, noble Mr. Steward!

LEERBEUTEL. Look, here are your jewels back. I don't think they came to any harm in my hand.

JEWELER. I'faith I won't take them back. I ask you most humbly to keep them till tomorrow.

LEERBEUTEL. No, I won't have them.

JEWELER. Then I hope the count won't hold it against me. *(Exit.)*

LEERBEUTEL. Heark'ee, Monsieur, as I see you didn't do this because you were suspicious, I'll let you leave them.

JEWELER. Thank you, Mr. Steward.

LEERBEUTEL. You can come here tomorrow at nine o'clock.

JEWELER. Very well. *(Exit.)*

Scene II

(Three town councilors; Leerbeutel)

First Councilor. Your humble servant, sir. I don't know whether you are one of the count's attendants.

Leerbeutel. Yes, I am, sir. I'm his steward, at your service. The count has taken the liberty of inviting you to supper and hopes you won't be offended.

Second Councilor. We are the count's humble servants and thank him for the honor he has done us.

Leerbeutel. His father, the old count, says that when he was young and he traveled abroad, he always was host to the authorities in each town, and he wants his dear son to do the same. The town council consists of men he can learn from and profit by. One shouldn't travel just to see houses and buildings, but to speak to decent folks as well.

First Councilor. We'd like to provide some entertainment here for his grace, but how can a gentleman of his social standing and education, who has traveled so much, profit by mixing with us? We can see from your politeness, intelligence, and manners how cultured your noble master must be.

Leerbeutel. I thank you most sincerely for your kind thoughts. My merits are very small, and unfortunately my master— Oh, dear sirs, I can't talk about it.

First Councilor. Why, Mr. Steward? We hope that nothing's happened to your master.

Leerbeutel. Kind gentlemen, nature has a very strange way of making her gifts. My master cannot complain of his physical appearance, everything is as it should be. He also has good health and is rich. But, dear sirs! *(He weeps bitterly.)* Oh, my heart bleeds when I think of it.

First Councilor. Maybe the count's a little frivolous. That's a fault of most young men like him. *(Leerbeutel cries again.)* But that will change as he grows older.

LEERBEUTEL. No, sir. If only he were a little wild and frivolous. That's a good sign in young men, I think.

FIRST COUNCILOR. Is he perhaps inclined to be sad?

LEERBEUTEL. No, I wish he were; sadness is usually mixed with something good.

FIRST COUNCILOR. Perhap's he's too fond of the girls and lets himself be led astray by them?

LEERBEUTEL. No, I wish he did; love has a lot of bad sides but also does a lot of good.

FIRST COUNCILOR. We can't think what's the matter. Is he perhaps harsh to his inferiors?

LEERBEUTEL. Certainly not. If only he could be a little strict. That's sometimes useful with such people.

FIRST COUNCILOR. His grace must have developed some strong tendencies.

LEERBEUTEL. No, kind gentlemen, neither strong or weak. He has no tendencies at all. When you see him, you'll swear he's no gentleman at all. You'd think he was a peasant boy rather than a count palatine. He's like a block of wood. He has no ideas and no memory, and all that his father has spent on him has been wasted. *(He cries again.)* Oh, that noble old count! When I think of the many salt tears he has shed, the many sighs he has breathed about this, my heart is ready to break. That kind gentleman has done everything a father can do for his child, has picked the best tutors in the country for him, the best drill-sergeants, and at last let him go abroad. But it's helped very little.

FIRST COUNCILOR. How old is the count now?

LEERBEUTEL. Nineteen.

FIRST COUNCILOR. Well, Mr. Steward, there's still hope; there are many examples of that.

LEERBEUTEL *(sighing)*. Oh, if only that were true. But excuse me, gentlemen, if I leave you a moment. I'll bring the gentleman down.

FIRST COUNCILOR. Your humble servant.

Scene 12

(The councilors, alone)

First Councilor. That steward's the best-hearted man, my dear colleague. He ought to have the rank of his master because of his great merits.

Second Councilor. Yes, you're right; I like him very much.

Third Councilor. I'm quite anxious to see the young count, if he's so foolish.

First Councilor. It must be a great sorrow for parents when their children don't yield to discipline. But he must be coming down now.

Scene 13

(The Count; Leerbeutel; the councilors; the landlord enters later)

First Councilor. Your humble servant. We thank your grace for the honor you have done us by inviting us here.

Second Councilor. If we'd known your grace was coming, we'd have had the honor long before this of paying our humble respects and congratulating you on your safe arrival.

Count. Have any of you kind gentlemen a pinch of snuff? I'm so stuffed up.

First Councilor *(aside)*. Good heavens! That's a fine way for a count to talk!

Leerbeutel. My dear sirs, the count has been lying down on the bed and fell asleep, and when he sleeps like that in the afternoon he gets so drowsy that it takes half an hour for him to recover. I ask you most humbly to sit down, and then my master will sit down too.

First Councilor *(aside)*. How clever that man is in hiding his master's weaknesses!

Leerbeutel. Oh, please sit down, gentlemen; his grace won't

sit before you do. *(The count sits down first, then the others. Leerbeutel remains standing by his chair.)*

FIRST COUNCILOR. Your grace has come to a very unhealthy place, so you must be careful at first and take some small precautions. *(The count belches.)*

LEERBEUTEL. The count has a terribly weak stomach and humbly begs your pardon for having to do this in your presence. Often he can't breathe, and so he takes this liberty, which he'd never do unless it was absolutely necessary.

FIRST COUNCILOR. His grace must feel free to do it. Health is the most precious jewel in the world. Has your grace been troubled long with these obstructions?

COUNT. Ask my steward.

FIRST COUNCILOR *(to the steward)*. Has his grace been troubled like this for long?

LEERBEUTEL. Yes, for several years.

SECOND COUNCILOR. I've some excellent drops here. If your grace would take them, I can assure you there's nothing better for the stomach.

COUNT. A dozen of those wouldn't make a half-pint. You can't quench your thirst that way.

LEERBEUTEL. Kind gentlemen, the count's not used to taking drops. He always uses a mixture and takes large draughts. He thought this was the mixture.

FIRST COUNCILOR. No, your grace, this isn't the mixture. You only take ten drops at a time.

COUNT. Ask my steward.

FIRST COUNCILOR. D'you know these drops, Mr. Steward?

LEERBEUTEL. I've only dabbled a little in medicine. Yes, I can tell at once from the smell what they are. It's a powerful tincture. You can't use much more than ten drops at a time.

FIRST COUNCILOR. But, your grace, how do you like this town?

COUNT. Ask my steward.

LEERBEUTEL. The count knows I've looked round the town

a little, so he thinks I could best describe it. He hasn't seen anything yet. I notice some beautiful and expensive buildings here.

First Councilor. Yes, the town is quite beautiful. It's grown the last few years. If the count would like to see the town, we'll do our very best to show him everything.

Leerbeutel. This politeness is so great that his grace can't find words strong enough to reply all at once. But his silence shows you how deeply he is moved.

First Councilor. You mustn't call it politeness. It's our duty to do it and anything else that can please the count.

Leerbeutel. What kind gentlemen you are! The count doesn't say much, but he thinks all the more. He gets that from his father who, when anyone does him a kindness, says nothing but shows his gratitude by his actions.

First Councilor. Is your grace's father still in good health?

Count. Ask my steward.

Leerbeutel. I must explain to you kind gentlemen that no one except me had a letter from the old count in the last mail, so his grace is a little put out, and when he refers you to me, he means to suggest in a subtle way that I was luckier in getting a letter than he was. On behalf of his grace I thank you for your inquiry. The old count and the countess, too, are both well.

First Councilor. Oh, is your grace's mother alive too?

Count. Ask my steward.

Leerbeutel. Ha, ha! You can easily see, gentlemen, that my master is still a little angry at not getting a letter from either of them by the last post. Oh, your grace must be calm. In the next mail your grace will have a letter and I won't get any.

Landlord *(enters)*. Everything's ready now, Mr. Steward; the food's on the table, if you'll be good enough to step inside. *(The count attempts to go in first, but Leerbeutel holds him back by his coat and makes the others enter before him.)*

LEERBEUTEL. Mr. Landlord, have the musicians come that I ordered?

LANDLORD. Yes, you'll hear the best music we have in town.

LEERBEUTEL. Tell them to play some nice pieces while the master is eating. *(The landlord tells the musicians to play. Some choice music is played, and a dancer enters and performs a beautiful dance.)*

SCENE 14

(Madame Staabi; the landlord)

MADAME STAABI. It's terribly quiet today. I can't see anyone, and it's after nine. But I can't believe they're all asleep. I must knock on the landlord's door.

LANDLORD *(coming out in his night-jacket with a belt on, rubbing his eyes)*. Good morning. You're out very early today.

MADAME STAABI. Is it early? It's nine o'clock.

LANDLORD *(yawning)*. Good heavens, is it nine o'clock? I didn't think it was so late. We drank a good deal last night, and my head feels as if it were crushed. The count treated us so well that we all got drunk. His steward is quite a gentleman and so gracious that I can't possibly describe it. He poured my drink out himself, that kind gentleman, and asked me to drink the count's health. I tell you the young count's going to be a fine gentleman. I'faith he drank level with the old councilors, but in the end he had to give up. I tell you, Madame Staabi, the count's still a young man, he's not twenty yet. How could he hold out against men who have sat on the council so many years?

MADAME STAABI. What sort of gentleman is he anyhow?

LANDLORD. He's very quiet. I hardly heard him say a word at the table. The steward did all the talking.

MADAME STAABI. Yes, that steward seems to be a polite man.

LANDLORD. I've never known such a man. I'll always speak

well of him. But excuse me, I must go in and wash and comb myself a bit. If you'll pardon me saying so, I just got out of bed. *(Exit.)*

Scene 15

(Madame Staabi; jeweler; a musician)

Madame Staabi. Your servant, Mr. Jeweler. Maybe you're here on the same business as myself.

Jeweler. Yes, the steward asked me to come at this time. I must thank you, Madame, for recommending me to him; I expect he'll keep the two jewels I left with him yesterday.

Musician. And I have to get some money for our performance yesterday.

Jeweler. Did they have a good time?

Musician. Yes, we had lots of music. The whole council was at the table. Will you kind gentlemen go in and speak to the count's servants?

Jeweler. Yes, I'd like my money for a couple of jewels.

Madame Staabi. And I want to be paid for thirty yards of brocade.

Musician. I'm not asking for nearly as much as you. You good folks can earn as much in an hour as people in our profession can in a year.

Jeweler. But, Monsieur, we don't always get such good pickings.

Madame Staabi. Yes, that's true enough.

Musician. But haven't any of the servants got up yet? I've very little time. I have to go off to a wedding at a shoemaker's, where we must blow the trumpets when the guests come. But here's the landlord; we must ask him.

Scene 16

(Jeweler; musician; Madame Staabi; landlord)

Musician. Mr. Landlord, can't you get us some of the count's people to talk to?

LANDLORD. I'faith I haven't seen any of them today.

JEWELER. Surely some of them must be up.

LANDLORD. I should imagine so. I'll go into the servants' room and wake them if they're not awake already. *(Exit.)*

MADAME STAABI. Isn't it terrible for servants to sleep so late?

MUSICIAN. They got to bed late last night, pretty tipsy, it's true, but still it's a bit too much for them to sleep so long.

LANDLORD *(entering)*. What the devil's all this? There's none of them in the room. They may be in with the steward, but I haven't seen his door open today.

JEWELER. Run in at once and look. Oh, I'm afraid there's something crooked going on here.

LANDLORD *(goes out and enters again)*. Oh, God help a poor miserable man! There's no one in the steward's room either.

JEWELER. Oh, all my blood's boiling.

MADAME STAABI. Oh, oh, I'm trembling.

LANDLORD. I must peep into the count's room. Ha, ha, what a relief! I see he's still lying there.

JEWELER. I can tell you, Mr. Landlord, I was as frightened as a rabbit.

LANDLORD. When people get frightened they'll imagine anything.

MADAME STAABI. It's a shame to suspect decent folks.

SCENE 17

(Peiter; the rest as before)

PEITER *(entering)*. Oh, master, what's happened? All our three horses have gone from the stable.

LANDLORD. What's that you're saying? Are you crazy?

PEITER. It's true, I tell you, master.

LANDLORD. Goodness gracious! If I hadn't seen the count asleep, I'd think something was wrong.

JEWELER. Mr. Landlord, don't stand here arguing any more, but go straight in to the count and wake him up without any more ceremony, and tell him that all his folks have gone and your horses as well. We must know what it's all about, whether he likes it or not.

LANDLORD *(opens the door to the bedroom and shouts).* Your grace, your grace, your grace!

SCENE 18

(The Count, in a dressing-gown and slippers; the others)

COUNT *(stretching himself).* Do you want to speak to me?

LANDLORD. I most humbly beg your pardon for troubling your grace, but—

COUNT. Go to my steward.

JEWELER. Gracious sir, we don't know where to find him. He asked me to come at this time, but—

COUNT. Didn't I tell you, go to the steward.

JEWELER. The steward isn't here, your grace.

COUNT. Call the valet then.

LANDLORD. We can't find him.

COUNT. He must be in with the steward. Go to the devil all of you and find that steward.

LANDLORD. The steward, the valet, the lackeys, the horses, everything's gone.

COUNT. What can I do about it?

JEWELER. If you'll pay me for my jewels, sir, the others can stay away as long as they like.

MADAME STAABI. And me for my thirty yards of brocade.

MUSICIAN. And me for entertaining you yesterday.

LANDLORD. And me for the food and the rest of the things that are gone.

COUNT. What have I to do with all that trash? Bad cess to you, go off to the steward.

LANDLORD. Where is the steward?

COUNT. What a silly devil you are! I've just got up and you want me to tell you where the steward is.

Jeweler. Mr. Landlord, I demand this person be arrested until I'm paid.

Landlord. Your grace must stay here till we're all paid. I see that your servants have all been in a plot. You must write to your father and tell him to send a few thousand dollars to get you free.

Count. My father! If only he had something to pay his rent with this year!

Landlord. What, aren't you a count?

Count. Count yourself! I'm the son of Peer Nielsen from Vigen.

Jeweler. Aren't you a count?

Count. They only called me that for a joke.

Landlord. Then how did you get all the servants and people you brought here yesterday?

Count. Ask the steward. How the devil do I know? I never saw him before yesterday when I came to town to buy tar. He said if I'd go with him and do what he told me I'd get good food and drink. I thanked him, and then he took off my country clothes and gave me a velvet coat and threw some hair dipped in flour on my head. He and everyone else called me count, which is a funny thing to call decent folks.

Landlord. Oh—oh! You wicked criminal, to swindle us so shamefully!

Count. Are you crazy? Have I swindled you?

Landlord. Wasn't it a swindle to pretend to be a count when you were only a peasant?

Count. There are sixteen peasants in our village who've all been May-kings, and the bailiff didn't do anything to them. Besides, this was done against my will. You made me a May-king yourselves, although it was not the custom; no one is a May-king except in the month of May.

Jeweler. Get me my precious stones again, you dog.

Count. Have you lost your stones? That's bad, you poor devil.

Madame Staabi *(crying)*. And my thirty yards of brocade.

Musician. I've got to be paid for my music, Mr. Landlord. I hold you responsible.

Landlord. Am I to pay for your playing, too? Haven't I been swindled enough?

Count. Let him go to the devil instead of paying him; he played like a rogue. Last summer, when I was the May-king, we had music with a drum too; here you didn't have even a decent country dance. I don't know what it was. It sounded like they were pinching cats' tails. One howled, then another, and then all of them together. If I was you, Mr. Landlord, they wouldn't get a penny.

Scene 19

(A councilor; the people from the former scene)

Councilor. Good morning, Mr. Landlord. Thank you for the party last night; you treated us very well.

Landlord. Yes, my purse is going to suffer.

Councilor. I've come to pay my most humble respects to the count and to thank him for last night.

Landlord. And I was on my way to pay my most humble respects to you and to ask that the count should be hanged before sunset.

Councilor. What does all this mean?

Landlord. It means that the count ought to be hanged. The steward was a rogue, the count has become a miserable peasant boy, I've been robbed, these other good folks have been swindled. Here he is. You can question him.

Councilor. Heark'ee, why did you pretend to be a count?

Count. Ask my steward.

Councilor. Where is he?

Landlord. He's gone off with three of my horses and all his baggage and left this poor peasant in the lurch.

COUNCILOR. Good heavens, what a story! You'll be hanged for certain; I never heard of such a trick.

COUNT. Devil take me if I don't tell the bailiff if you hang me, and then he'll hang you.

COUNCILOR. Take him off to the town hall; the case is clear. *(They drag him away.)*

SCENE 20

(The peasant boy's parents; the people from the former scene)

MOTHER. I didn't want to send that simple boy to the town.

FATHER. But he must go to the market town sometime so as to learn something.

MOTHER. Oh, what could that foolish creature learn? I'm so frightened he'll be taken for a soldier.

FATHER. If we don't find him, we'll have to pay Mr. Mark to make inquiries for him, and if we do that from the pulpit, the officer who's taken him will give him back.

MOTHER. So you say! Of course the officers give their soldiers back!

FATHER. I hope nothing worse has happened to him than being taken in the army. I'm afraid, Gertrude, he may have got into worse trouble.

MOTHER. Oh, oh, he's our only son after all, and however foolish he is, he's still useful to us in our work.

FATHER. If he's gone, Gertrude, we must put up with it.

MOTHER. I'll never be happy. You must get the boy back or give me another son in his place.

FATHER. You'll have to get someone else to do that; I'm too old and weak to give you any more children. *(She cries.)* Don't cry now, my child. We'll look for him on the new farm. Maybe he'll be there.

MOTHER. Nonsense, why should he go there?

FATHER. We'll go over there anyhow. But what's all that noise about? In these market towns you see nothing but evil.

They're dragging a prisoner away. *(To the councilor.)* Excuse me, kind sir, what has that man done?

Councilor. They're going to hang him.

Boy. I'll be damned if that's not my parents. Oh, my dear parents, you've just come at the right time to follow me to the gallows.

Mother. Husband, it's our son Peer Nielsen.

Father. I'faith I believe it is. Peer Nielsen, what's the matter? What have you done wrong?

Boy. Oh, dear father, don't be angry with me; I've lost the twopence you gave me to buy tar with.

Councilor. Oh, what simplicity! I feel sorry for him. Heark'ee, good man, is that your son?

Father *(crying)*. Yes, gracious sir. But why should my son be hanged?

Councilor. He pretended to be a great man and caused these good people who are standing here to lose their property.

Mother. Oh, that's impossible, gracious sir, he's the simplest person on earth. Is it true you are charged with this?

Boy. Devil take that steward! If only I could get hold of him!

Councilor. How did you get to know the steward?

Boy. When I stood in the market yesterday looking round, he came up to me and said: "If you'll come with me and do what I tell you, you'll be better off than your master and mistress." I would have been an idiot not to say yes to this. I went along with him. He put a velvet coat on me, called me count, took me in this man's house, and he called me count too, and gave me enough food and drink to last me a whole year. I go to bed and don't think about anything. In the morning they say I'm going to be hanged because I was a count yesterday. The devil take their counts the next time!

Mother *(crying)*. You can see how simple he is, kind sir, and that he's not the one to do anything wrong. Other folks have used his simple nature and made him a tool to cheat people. Have pity on me and don't send me to an early grave.

Councilor. What do you say, you good folks who have been swindled? Would it help you if this simple soul was sacrificed when he was innocent?

Jeweler. It wouldn't help us at all. I feel sorry for him myself.

Boy. I'll gladly pay for what has happened. One of them has lost two stones; I'll give him ten.

Councilor. I feel that the boy is innocent and more deserving of pity than punishment. No law allows us to punish him as an innocent tool, but we must give him back to his parents with a warning that they should not let him go to town any more alone, so that no tragic events like this can happen again.

CONSCIENCE. What do you say, you good folks who have been swindled? Would it help you if this simple soul was sacrificed when he was innocent?

JUSTICE. It wouldn't help us at all. I feel sorry for him myself.

DEV. I'll gladly pay for what has happened. One of them has lost two geese; I'll give him ten.

CONSCIENCE. I feel that the boy is innocent and more deserving of pity than punishment. No law allows us to punish him as an innocent soul, but we must give him back to his parents with a warning that they should not let him go to town any more alone, so that no tragic events like this can happen again.

Sganarel's Journey
to
The Land of the Philosophers

[SGANARELS REJSE TIL DET FILOSOFISKE LAND]

A COMEDY IN ONE ACT

1751

DRAMATIS PERSONÆ

SGANAREL, *a servant*
LEANDER, *his master*
PHILOSOPHERS OF VARIOUS SCHOOLS
A DOCTOR OF MEDICINE
MARGARET, *the doctor's wife*
LUCIE, AGATHA, *two wives of philosophers*
POLYPHEMUS

SGANAREL'S JOURNEY TO THE LAND OF THE PHILOSOPHERS

Scene 1

(Sganarel alone, his hands raised)

Sganarel. Heaven be praised that at last, after so much trouble, we've come to the town we've been looking for and where we are considering settling down. What could be more delightful than to live among pure philosophers and listen to nothing but wisdom? I'm tired and exhausted from the journey, but when I see our goal is at hand I seem to get fresh strength again. My master Leander, who is outside the gate with the carriage, has sent me on ahead to get lodgings. But I don't see any people; it's as quiet here as if it were nighttime. So I must knock at the first door to find somebody to speak to. *(He knocks.)*

Scene 2

(Sganarel; a philosopher with a long beard)

Sganarel. There's someone coming. Wisdom is written on his forehead. Master, I hope you won't be offended if I ask if you know of a lodging for two strangers. *(The philosopher does not answer; he merely yawns.)* Perhaps you didn't hear my question, Doctor. *(The philosopher is silent and yawns again.)* I asked if you knew of some good lodgings for two travelers.

Philosopher *(yawns for the third time, looks at the sun, and says)*. According to the sun it must be nine o'clock.

Sganarel. I didn't ask about the time of the sun. I was asking about lodgings. *(The philosopher yawns for the fourth time and goes off.)*

Sganarel *(yawning in his turn)*. If this fellow is a wise man, he's not much use, as he doesn't talk but just yawns out wisdom. But I must see if I can get hold of another who talks a little more and yawns a little less. *(He knocks at another door.)*

Scene 3

(Sganarel; a Heraclitic philosopher)

Philosopher. Do you want to speak to me?

Sganarel. I'm a stranger, and my master and I have come to this town after a troublesome and arduous journey. We've put up patiently with all the inconveniences of the journey in the hope that— *(The philosopher howls and cries.)* The tears you shed, doctor, are a proof of your noble heart and your sympathy, but now everything is forgotten, as— *(The philosopher cries again.)* I say everything's forgotten. Now all I ask is that you should get us good lodgings, which we'll pay for. *(The philosopher cries again, and Sganarel says, in an aside).* This man is as crazy as the first one.

Philosopher. What do you mean by the first one?

Sganarel. The first man I asked talked back at random, so I was quite puzzled.

Philosopher *(cries again, and Sganarel imitates him).* You say you were quite puzzled?

Sganarel. Yes, what else could I be when— *(The philosopher cries again, and Sganarel hits him on the behind. They both cry.)* Now you have something to cry about. What devilish faces these philosophers pull! But there's another one going across the street. He looks happy and agreeable. I expect I'll get some information from him about this mystery.

Scene 4

(Sganarel; a Democratic philosopher)

Sganarel. May I have a word with you, Right Reverend Sir?

Philosopher. Yes, of course, talk as much as you like.

SGANAREL *(aside)*. This man's very polite. *(Aloud.)* A lot of strange things have happened to me.

PHILOSOPHER. How's that?

SGANAREL. I talked to two philosophers here. I asked the first one if he knew of any lodgings, but instead of answering my question he just yawned and then said it was nine o'clock. Can that man be right in his head?

PHILOSOPHER. Ha, ha, hee, hee, ha, ha, ha!

SGANAREL. Yes, Master, you've good reason to laugh. I can hardly stop laughing myself when I think of it. *(They both laugh.)*

PHILOSOPHER. But what did the other one answer?

SGANAREL. The other cried whenever I asked him anything and howled as if he had been whipped.

PHILOSOPHER. Ha, ha, ha! Hee, hee, ha, ha!

SGANAREL. I thought he was just as crazy as the first one. *(They laugh heartily again.)* What can you think of such people?

PHILOSOPHER. Ha, ha, ha! Hee, hee, ha, ha! I see from your appearance and clothing that you're a stranger.

SGANAREL. Yes, Master, from a distant land.

PHILOSOPHER. A distant land? Ha, ha, hee, ha!

SGANAREL. That's nothing to laugh at.

PHILOSOPHER. What's your business here?

SGANAREL. To mix with learned men and to be taught wisdom. *(The philosopher laughs again.)* Oh, sir, try to keep that laughing down and let's have a serious talk.

PHILOSOPHER. A serious talk, did you say? Ha, ha!

SGANAREL. What the devil's all this about? Just stop laughing for a bit and tell me where I can find a good lodging.

PHILOSOPHER. A good lodging, did you say? *(He goes off laughing.)*

SGANAREL. All right, laugh your head off, you brute. One philosopher is crazier than another. I'm so bewildered by all this that I don't know whether I'm asleep or awake. If this is the city of wisdom, I'd like to know what a madhouse is. Now I must put it all together so I can tell my master the whole thing in detail.

Scene 5

(Sganarel; another philosopher who, while Sganarel stands there thinking, enters at full speed and runs him down so that he falls over)

Sganarel. Bad cess to you, what does that mean? Why do you treat me like that? What have I done wrong?

Philosopher *(lifting him up by his legs)*. Oh, oh, I'm taking your legs instead of your arms. I ask you a thousand pardons. It's because my sight's too good.

Sganarel. I should think it's because you are as blind as a bat.

Philosopher. Sir, because of the strong sight that nature has given me I cannot see anything that is near.

Sganarel. If nature couldn't give you anything except that, you must wish she'd kept it to herself.

Philosopher. No, sir. I can see what others can't; my strong eyesight goes right inside a thing and seizes on its essence, which is hidden from other people.

Sganarel. That's beyond me.

Philosopher. But it's true, sir. That's why I'm called the subtle doctor. But I see you're a stranger. What have you come here for? If I can help you in any way, I'd be glad.

Sganarel. Thank you very much. To begin with I might ask if it's possible to get some good lodgings here for two people.

Philosopher. I don't bother with such common, crude things, but if you would like to know something about *philosophia occulta*, I'm at your service.

Sganarel. No, no, I'm only asking about—

Philosopher. For instance, the power of the magnet, the

nature of the soul, the circulation of the blood, the characteristics of ants and gnats, the internal form of other insects, the—

SGANAREL. No, no, for heaven's sake no! I'm only asking if—

PHILOSOPHER. Or do you want to know something about the souls of animals, whether they are machines or living creatures, whether *nominales* or *reales* should be called orthodox philosophy? *(As he is talking, Sganarel runs him down and he too apologizes because of his sharp eyesight. The subtle philosopher gets up again at once, knocks Sganarel onto the ground, gives him some sound blows, and leaves him lying there.)*

SCENE 6

(Sganarel; an astrologer looking through a telescope)

SGANAREL. Oh, oh, won't anyone help me up? Oh, help a poor, injured man, who can't get up.

ASTROLOGER *(looking around)*. Who's that calling? There's a man lying there half dead. What's the matter, my friend?

SGANAREL. Help me up again, sir. I've fallen into the hands of wicked men; they've beaten me so badly that my limbs are crushed.

ASTROLOGER. I'm very sorry. My duty is to help my neighbor; I only ask for a little patience till I look in my astrological book to see if in this month and on this day of the month I may do anything important. *(Turns over the pages of the book.)* No, sir, this is not the right time. I see it's the fourteenth day of the month of Morian, and according to astrological rules you can do nothing then. If you'll be patient, sir, till the sun goes down, I'll be able to help you without breaking the rules of astrology.

SGANAREL. The devil must have dictated those rules. Can there really be a time when it's forbidden to help your neighbor?

ASTROLOGER. Of course there can be and there is.

Sganarel. Oh, what a miserable man I am! It was an unhappy day when we decided to come to this town.

Astrologer. Don't say that, sir. You've come to a place where the nine muses have their seat.

Sganarel. You should rather say nine goddesses of hell or nine misfortunes, as—

Astrologer. Don't be too hasty. Calm your passions and be patient till tonight, and I'll be glad to help you. Goodbye for now. *(Exit.)*

Scene 7

(Sganarel; a Skeptic philosopher)

Sganarel. Oh, oh, isn't there a sympathetic soul in this whole town?

Philosopher. I hear someone calling. I see a poor man there who's been hurt. *(He lifts Sganarel up.)*

Sganarel. A thousand thanks, Doctor. I'm glad to find an honest or a wise man in this learned city.

Philosopher. What's the trouble, my friend?

Sganarel. I've been beaten and brutally handled by one of your colleagues, who called himself a subtle philosopher, but he didn't seem to see much that was subtle in me.

Philosopher. But are you sure about this?

Sganarel. Shouldn't I be sure about something that has just happened?

Philosopher. Your senses may have deceived you.

Sganarel. Well, my feelings didn't deceive me. My bruised limbs are proof of that.

Philosopher. Your feelings, one of the five senses, can deceive you just like your eyes.

Sganarel. That's confounded nonsense. You yourself saw that I was lying on the ground calling for help.

Philosopher. It seemed so to me, but—

Sganarel. Bad cess to you with your "but." Didn't you help me up yourself?

Philosopher. That may be.

Sganarel. So I can take my thanks back.

Philosopher. Maybe.

Sganarel. Maybe, maybe! Heark'ee, my good "maybe." If anyone treated you like that, what would you say?

Philosopher. I would only say it seemed to be so. *(Sganarel gives him three good blows.)* Ouch! That's a disgraceful way to treat a philosopher.

Sganarel. Maybe.

Philosopher. And to reward good deeds.

Sganarel. Maybe, maybe.

Philosopher. Oh, my poor back!

Sganarel. Your feelings are one of the five senses and can deceive you as well as your eyes.

Philosopher. I must go home at once and put some ointment on my back.

Sganarel. Go to Jericho and put ointment on your learned brain. It needs it more than your back. If I wasn't expecting my master Leander any moment, I'd run off at once to avoid any more annoyances. If he'd only hurry! But I see him coming now. I'll give him everything just as fresh as I got it.

Scene 8

(Leander; Sganarel)

Leander. Well, how goes it, Sganarel? Have you found good lodgings? *(Sganarel does not answer; he just yawns.)* Didn't you hear what I said? *(He yawns again.)* I believe he's gone both blind and dumb. *(He yawns again.)* Don't stand there making fun of me. Can't you answer my question?

Sganarel. What d'you want to know, sir?

Leander. I asked you if you'd found any lodgings.

Sganarel *(looking up at the sky and yawning)*. I see by the sun it's nine o'clock.

Leander. What the devil's all this? The fellow must be

bewitched. Don't you know me? *(Sganarel howls and cries.)* Just tell me where you've been and what has happened to you. *(He cries again.)* Oh, this is unfortunate. *(He cries again.)* Don't you know me; I'm your master.

SGANAREL. My master? Ha, ha, hee, hee, ha!

LEANDER. I see he's lost his mind.

SGANAREL. Ha, ha, hee, hee!

LEANDER. Is this the result of the air in this town?

SGANAREL. Ha, ha! No, sir, my mind's all right, but I can't answer your question exactly.

LEANDER. Can't you say yes or no?

SGANAREL. Maybe.

LEANDER. What d'you mean by "maybe"?

SGANAREL. Nothing of any importance.

LEANDER. If you're making fun of me, you'll be sorry for it.

SGANAREL. I'm not making fun of you at all, sir.

LEANDER. Isn't it making fun when you talk at random whenever I ask a question?

SGANAREL. It only seems so, sir; you mustn't rely on the senses; they're all deceptive.

LEANDER *(raising his cane)*. No, that's going too far.

SGANAREL. That's going too far as well. Now I'll speak a little more seriously and tell you that it was an unfortunate hour when we decided to make this trip. All these compliments I've been paying you, sir, are the same as I got from all the philosophers I spoke to. I give them to you as cordially as I received them. The town is full of idiots who are crammed with learning.

LEANDER. I thought learning and wisdom went together.

SGANAREL. So did I.

LEANDER. I never heard anything else.

SGANAREL. But I felt something else.

LEANDER. How can such a thing happen?

SGANAREL. You spoil everything if you have too much of it. A glass of wine cheers you up, but if you drink too much of it, the brain is philosophically upset. The wind drives the ship along, but if it blows too hard, you turn over. No food is healthier than meal-pudding, but if you load up your stomach with too much of it, you can get a fever. That's how it is with these philosophers. Too much learning has turned them crazy.

LEANDER. According to that we would have been better off at home.

SGANAREL. That's what I think. But there's some women coming along. They seem to be very human and domesticated.

LEANDER. Let's stand aside and see how they behave.

SCENE 9

(Agatha; Lucie and Margaret; Sganarel; Leander)

AGATHA. Oh, sister, I long so much to see the stranger who's just come here.

LUCIE. So do I. I've heard he's a very nice man.

MARGARET. I'm already deeply in love before I've seen him.

AGATHA. My maid has seen him and says he's a second Paris.

LUCIE. If he's Paris, I'd like to be Helen. But look, there's two men now. They must be the ones we're going crazy about.

AGATHA. I'm sure they're the same. They look very different from our moldy, rusty philosophers.

LUCIE. You're quite right there, sister. Just look at that one's nice curly hair.

AGATHA. Look, what a figure!

LUCIE. What nice legs the other one has! They make my mouth water. We must talk to them at once.

MARGARET. Welcome to town, kind men. What are you doing here?

SGANAREL. Before we answer, we must know if you are philosophers or human beings.

LUCIE. We're certainly human, we know that much. Sisters, they think we're not human.

AGATHA. We're not only human but we're also docile and obliging, especially towards strangers.

LUCIE. You might say that twice, sister. Ha, ha! What a funny question: are we human?

SGANAREL. Good! Then I may tell you that we've come here to ask about some good lodgings. We consulted some philosophers about it, but one answered at random, the other treated me to some tears, the third laughed, and the fourth wanted to look at the heavens to see what answer he ought to make.

MARGARET. My dear friends, don't take any notice of them. Their studies have made them crazy. We, unfortunately, find this every day, as we're their wives.

LEANDER. Are you their wives?

MARGARET. Yes, we're called that, but— *(They all sigh and weep.)*

LEANDER. What do you mean, that you are just called that?

MARGARET. They study so deeply that they neglect the most urgent things. They forget what is most important, the duty of a husband. Isn't that so, sister?

AGATHA. Yes, that's true. *(All three weep bitterly.)*

LEANDER. What d'you mean by the duty of a husband?

LUCIE. You tell him, sister, you've been married longest.

AGATHA. Let Margaret tell them.

MARGARET. Let Lucie tell.

LEANDER. I know what you mean, my dear children.

AGATHA. If some strange traveler didn't help us out a little now and then, we'd pass away entirely. Isn't that true, sister?

LUCIE. Yes, too true. *(They weep sadly once again.)*

LEANDER. But do your husbands allow you to mix freely with strangers?

MARGARET. Our husbands? We can fool them as much as we want.

LEANDER. If that's the case, of course you kind ladies will be helped.

MARGARET. I thank you a thousand times.

Sganarel. Master, now I'll have great pleasure in staying here. All we have to do is to get some good lodgings.

Margaret. If you kind gentlemen will be satisfied with our house, it's at your service.

Sganarel. But your husband is a philosopher too.

Margaret. Yes, but not one of those you've been talking about. He's a doctor of medicine. Those sort of people don't study much; their practice doesn't allow them to read a lot. I'm sure you'll be well received by my husband. Just come in with me and everything will be settled soon. *(She takes them in.)*

Scene 10

(Agatha; Lucie)

Agatha. My dear sister, weren't they two delightful men? Which did you like best?

Lucie. I liked them both, especially the one with the curly hair. I'faith he was a dainty morsel.

Agatha. I liked the other just as well.

Lucie. They seem to have come from far-off countries. You could see that by their faces and gestures.

Agatha. But what can they want here?

Lucie. The same as other strangers who think they will find wisdom here, as the town is full of philosophers and is even called the city of wisdom.

Agatha. Then they won't find what they're looking for.

Lucie. You're right, sister. It's one thing to be learned and another to be wise. What's the use of learning if it distorts people's minds?

Agatha. My husband is so carried away by his studies that he often sits at the table without eating and gets up still hungry, imagining that he is full.

Lucie. My husband has just as funny habits.

Agatha. Our medical doctors are a little more decent than

the rest because they don't study so much and mix more with other folks.

Lucie. That's true enough. But some of them are crotchety too. So I'm longing to know whether the visitors will be satisfied with that doctor. But there they are coming out again. I'm afraid they got a poor reception. Let's go off and tell our neighbors' wives what we've seen. *(Exeunt.)*

Scene II

(Leander; Sganarel)

Leander. That man's very polite and decent. He not only offered us his house, but did so without asking payment.

Sganarel. Now I'm beginning to recover again, as I see there are learned people without eccentricities.

Leander. The rest of his colleagues were also civilized.

Sganarel. I think they are all medical doctors.

Leander. Yes, our host told me that the whole faculty of medicine was collected in his house and that was why he couldn't talk to us any longer at this time. But one thing puzzles me. I can't understand why they looked at us so carefully and whispered together so much.

Sganarel. It's only because our appearance and our clothes are so strange and unusual.

Leander. I suppose it might be that. But—

Sganarel. Oh, sir, you're worrying about nothing. For my part I'm very pleased we've got such good lodgings. But I see the women have all gone.

Leander. I expect they've gone to announce our arrival to the neighbors' wives.

Sganarel. As I see it, a stranger can enjoy himself here with these wives of learned men; they're all very obliging. But here's our hostess coming with a bottle of wine.

Scene 12

(Margaret; Leander; Sganarel)

MARGARET. My dear men, I hope it isn't too slow for you here. As soon as my husband is finished with the faculty and his colleagues have gone, he will have the honor of another talk with you. Meanwhile he's asked me to keep you company. *(She pours a glass of wine and gives it to Leander, at the same time sighing and weeping.)*

LEANDER. What's the matter, Madame? Why do you sigh so deeply?

SGANAREL *(aside)*. I feel sure she's going to say she's in love. *(She pours another glass for Sganarel, sighing and weeping the same as before.)*

LEANDER. My dear lady, you must tell me what's causing you this distress. *(She sighs and weeps again.)* Tell us what it's about. I'm burning to know.

MARGARET. Kind sirs, you've come to a decent house.

LEANDER. I'm sure of that.

MARGARET. My husband is known as one of the most upright and obliging men in this town.

LEANDER. There's no doubt about that, ma'am.

MARGARET. But he'll spare neither expense or trouble when he sees he can get a more exact knowledge of medicine and improve this art. When he saw you two nice gentlemen and your unusual appearance, he decided to dissect you both—not out of spite but purely to throw light on some medical problems.

SGANAREL. What does that mean—dissect?

LEANDER. It means—have your belly cut open.

SGANAREL. What—let them cut my belly open?

MARGARET. I can assure you it's not out of spite. He has a very kind heart for strangers.

SGANAREL. He must have the devil in him rather than a

kind heart when he wants to cut up a decent fellow. This is a fine trip we made, Master.

LEANDER. But are you serious, Madame, or are you joking with us?

MARGARET. It's quite settled. I almost fainted when I heard it.

LEANDER. But can't you plead for us and prevent this?

MARGARET. No, it's decided by the vote of the majority in the faculty. You know the doctors never change their minds, especially when the whole faculty have decided.

SGANAREL *(crying)*. Isn't there any magistrate we can appeal to?

MARGARET. The magistrate is the town physician and he never stops the doctors doing something that is intended to throw light on the subject of anatomy.

SGANAREL. This is a fine trip we made, sir.

LEANDER *(kneeling)*. Oh, Madame, think of some way to rescue two innocent men.

SGANAREL *(also kneeling)*. Oh, Madame, have pity on us! I've only one belly and I can't spare it.

MARGARET. Listen, my dear friends. If you'll take me and my sisters, who are married to two philosophers, with you, and bring us to your own country, we'll all run off together. Just stand up and stay here till I get them; they're as tired of their husbands as I am of mine.

SGANAREL. Don't stay away long, Madame. *(Exit Margaret.)*

SCENE 13

(Leander; Sganarel)

SGANAREL. It was a devil of an idea to settle down in this philosophers' town.

LEANDER. You see from this that all that glitters is not gold. I've no doubt the town is swarming with learned men, but it doesn't look as if their life corresponds to their learning. A lot of people study just to know more but not to be more wise.

SGANAREL. You might say, sir, they study just to go crazy.

A town like this should be uprooted and all its people destroyed.

LEANDER. You might better say given a little bloodletting or put in a madhouse, for it's not wickedness but just too much learning that's driven them crazy.

SGANAREL. Isn't it wickedness to want to cut decent folks' bellies? I seem to feel the knife already in mine.

LEANDER. I admit that those people should be destroyed, but the others are only laughable. I notice too that these philosophers can be divided into different sects. The one who cried must follow Heraclitus, the one that laughed Democritus, and the one who doubted everything must be a skeptic.

SGANAREL. Which of them is the craziest?

LEANDER. They're all as crazy as each other, though in different ways. But we must admire the women.

SGANAREL. Yes, especially if they keep their promise.

LEANDER. I'm hoping they will. I notice they're not satisfied with those philosophers.

SGANAREL. If only they would hurry up! Every moment seems as long as a day to me.

LEANDER. Patience, Sganarel! All we can depend on is their help. Feminine cunning is great, and it's not hard to fool men who are lost in the clouds.

SGANAREL. If I escape this danger successfully, I'll get busy and make life miserable for all philosophers.

LEANDER. Not all, but only those who misuse philosophy. For just as some of them are perverted by its misuse, so its proper use improves and civilizes others. But I see those kind women coming along.

SCENE 14

(Leander; Sganarel; Margaret, Agatha and Lucie, carrying small cases in their arms; Polyphemus)

MARGARET. I suppose it seemed a long time to you, my dear friends.

Leander. We counted every minute.

Sganarel. And I every second.

Margaret. Now we depend on your promises not to leave us when we reach a safe place.

Leander. We shall be grateful to you for this as long as we live.

Margaret. These boxes, full of gold and jewels, are going with us.

Sganarel. Now I can breathe again and I no longer have a pain in my guts.

Leander. But, dear ladies, I'm afraid your husbands will pursue us at once and then we'll be worse off in the end.

Margaret *(pointing to Polyphemus)*. We've brought this cunning fellow with us; he's always on hand when we want to cheat those philosophers.

Polyphemus. I'll certainly think up some way of stopping them from following you.

Leander. But what way?

Polyphemus. I can't tell you. Just rely on me and don't trouble your heads. First of all let's hide in this corner till the storm is over. *(They hide in a corner.)*

Scene 15

(The doctor and the three philosophers, who come in one after the other)

Doctor *(entering at full speed)*. What a misfortune this is! I can't find the strangers any more, nor my wife, and my box has been broken open. Hi, hi, where are you? My whole body is shaking and trembling. My wife must have told them the plans of the faculty and run off with them. Oh, heavens! what a disaster! I can say I never wanted to dissect anyone more than those two men, especially the one with the cloak, for I felt that his interior construction would throw a great deal of light on the science of anatomy.

First Philosopher *(at full speed).* Oh—oh—oh! I'm ruined! My money-box is gone and I can't find my wife anywhere.

Second Philosopher *(entering in the same way).* Hi, hi! Help me, anyone who can! My cupboard's broken open, and my treasure, that was dearer to me than my life, is gone. Oh, what a wretched man I am! If I don't get my treasures back, I'll hang myself in despair.

Third Philosopher *(comes rushing in).* Hi, hi, hi, stop that thief! I've been robbed. All my boxes have been opened and the one I kept my gold and jewels in has gone. Where's my wife? There's no time to be lost. I must rush off to the town gate. *(He runs and knocks the others down. They get up again, clasp their hands, and shout and cry.)* What's the matter, my dear brothers?

Doctor. Two strange thieves who came to my house just now have run off with my wife and my money.

Third Philosopher. The same thing has happened to me.

Doctor. This isn't the first time our wives have deceived us. We must call the police at once to chase them.

Scene 16

(Polyphemus enters and falls prostrate)

Doctor. This is our good friend Polyphemus. What misfortune could have happened to him? Maybe he's been robbed too. Heark'ee, Polyphemus, what's wrong?

Polyphemus. Oh, what an adventure! What a sight!

Doctor. Get up! Don't you know us?

Polyphemus. Oh, what a strange sight! It's got me so dazed I can't see anything clearly.

Doctor. Tell us what you saw.

Polyphemus. A moment ago, when I was out in the field, I saw two people in strange clothes, and three matrons with them. They waved to me, and when I got near, one of them said: "Go back at once to the town and tell them what you've seen. I'm Jupiter and this person is Mercury. We've taken human form and come down from heaven to carry off these three virtuous matrons and put them among the goddesses, as I feel they're too good to live any longer among sinful human beings." Then he went on: "Tell their husbands they sinned against heaven with the harsh words they uttered against the highest of the goddesses, and that this sin must be expiated by going home at once and fasting and praying for three days. After that, to honor Jupiter and Mercury, they must establish an annual festival, to be called The Feast of the Abduction." When he had said this, they all began to shine like the sun and rose up through the air.

ALL THE PHILOSOPHERS *(raising their hands and calling). O, magnum miraculum.*

POLYPHEMUS. I can still catch a glimpse of them. Just look up in the sky to the right, where I'm pointing.

A PHILOSOPHER *(crying).* That's quite true; I can see a glimpse of it too. My dear brothers, let's go home at once and carry out the wish of heaven. *(They kneel and sing):*

FIRST PHILOSOPHER. *O felices animae! vivae in coelum raptae.*

ALL. *Orate pro nobis.*

SECOND PHILOSOPHER. *Quas dignatus Jupiter reddere immortales.*

ALL. *Orate pro nobis.*

THIRD PHILOSOPHER. *O novae coelicolae! Lucia, Margaretha cum dilecta Agatha.*

ALL. *Orate pro nobis. (They get up and go off.)*

SCENE 17

(Polyphemus; Leander; Sganarel; the three women)

POLYPHEMUS. You can come out again now. You see from the trick I played how you can deceive those learned fellows who've been carried away by their studies.

LEANDER. When people get to know about this, there'll be a big fuss; it can't be kept quiet long.

POLYPHEMUS. Everything can be revealed when we are safe. Then one philosopher will moderate his laughter, the other will have a good reason for crying, and the third won't deny the evidence of his senses any more. *(They all thank him and then they sing the following song.)*

FIRST WOMAN:

Farewell, my philosophic land;
  My back to you I'll turn.
A better man will hold my hand
  Where people less do learn.
Where woman's endless troubles cease,
  No more a prey to man's caprice.

SECOND WOMAN:

Democritus no longer laughs,
  But rather tears must shed
As often as the sense of this
  Gets through his misty head.
Heraclitus has cause to cry
  For ever and a day.
The tears bedew his cheeks and beard
  As he observes this play.

THIRD WOMAN:

Pyrrhus could never see the truth
  Though he looked closely out,
But after this he'll never dare
  To mock folk with his doubt.
My Stoic spouse no longer can
  With learning us defy,
Emotion's language contradict,
  And passion's strength deny.

With my two sisters I am sure
  I always shall agree
That in this trick a lesson deep
  Our astrologue can see.
For though he knows what's in the sky
  And is with learning crammed,
In earthly things he has no skill,
  A foolish coward, damned.

LEANDER:

From this account we surely can
  Deduce as clear as day
That beard and cloak on any man
  No dividends will pay.

SGANAREL:

I'll drop my sorrow now for aye
  And join in the refrain.
A hundred times to Heaven I'll pray
  And my stomach I'll retain.

The Changed Bridegroom

[DEN FORVANDLEDE BRUDGOM]

A COMEDY IN ONE ACT

(FOR ACTRESSES ALONE)

1753

DRAMATIS PERSONÆ

FRU TERENTIA
PERNILLE
LEONORA, LAURENTIA, *Fru Terentia's daughters*
KIRSTEN THE MARRIAGE-MAKER *(a disguised actress)*
ELSEBET *(disguised as a captain)*

THE CHANGED BRIDEGROOM

Scene i

(Fru Terentia, dressed up and painted; Pernille)

Terentia. Heark'ee, Pernille. I've something important to tell you.

Pernille. I can guess what it is: you are going to catechize me as usual. That's all right, but there's reason in everything.

Terentia. Did you say catechize?

Pernille. Yes, that's what they call it. I mean your curtain lectures, that you work so hard at every day.

Terentia. You are wrong, Pernille. I'm going to give you quite a different kind of lecture; since I was in the capital for a few weeks I've become another person. Now the only speeches that I like are about engagements, weddings, dances, games, and masquerades.

Pernille. Well, I feel quite unhappy. If that's the case, you ought to belong to Ovid's *Metamorphosis*. And your clothes and frizzy hair make me think you're completely changed since you came back. Your face doesn't have that catechizing look and your eyes sparkle as if you might have fallen in love.

Terentia. That's just what has happened, Pernille.

Pernille. It's like seeing a tree budding in winter when the leaves usually fall. I can't believe that you intend to get married in your old age.

Terentia. What? Old age? That's a devil of an idea! Certainly I'm going to get married.

Pernille. Nonsense! I'll never believe it.

Terentia. Upon my soul I'm getting married. Won't you believe it?

Pernille. To whom then? I suppose it's our opposite neighbor, old Jeronimus, who calls in so often.

Terentia. Old Jeronimus! A thousand times no! I don't

like antiques; I want young blood. I like officers best. I'm crazy about those young soldiers.

PERNILLE. Ha, ha, ha—

TERENTIA. You can laugh, Pernille. When I was last in town I met three young cavaliers with ostrich plumes. They were such delightful company that I felt I'd like to marry all three of them if it had been allowed. But I liked one best of all; I tell you he was such a dainty tidbit, he looked like a beautiful girl.

PERNILLE. I'm very pleased with this talk, but I still hope it's all a joke.

TERENTIA. I can assure you on my honor that it's perfectly serious. I want to get married, and I'll marry a man like that.

PERNILLE. If it is serious, Madame, then you no longer have any honor to protest about—such conduct means it is gone. Just think what this means: it's something that will cause laughter and scorn—why, there's nothing funnier in a comedy. And think too how your two daughters will feel when they get to know they are going to have a prying young fellow as a stepfather.

TERENTIA. I don't care about people's talk or my daughters' anger.

PERNILLE. And remember too, Madame, that—

TERENTIA. I don't want to hear anything more against it. I only ask you to be loyal to me.

PERNILLE. It's not loyal to support you in something that will disgrace and ruin you.

TERENTIA. I only ask you, first of all, not to say anything about this till I've talked it over with old Madame Kirsten the matchmaker, who is used to helping people in love.

PERNILLE. You don't often recommend a young girl to be silent. I must speak about it, if it comes out of my sides.

TERENTIA. Look, Pernille, here's ten ducats for you if you'll keep quiet and help me.

PERNILLE. I admit that's very tempting, but—

TERENTIA. No buts! Just take the money.

PERNILLE. I see I'm to humor you, Madame.

TERENTIA. If you keep your promise, you'll get twice as much later on. Now I'm off to consult Madame Kirsten. *(Exit Terentia.)*

SCENE 2

(Pernille alone)

Am I asleep or dreaming? Am I in my right mind? Can such a change be natural? If anyone else had told me that this nice, pious Terentia had become foolish and sensuous, and that an old hurdy-gurdy like her would begin to run after young men, I'd have thought it the most fantastic story. But I must believe what my own ears have heard and is sworn to. I remember reading in some author that certain people get younger in their old age and that they begin to go crazy before they get gray hair. When I think about it I can find several examples of this, so I notice that even if it doesn't happen all the time, it's not quite unnatural. That trip to the capital that Madame made must certainly have caused this; she's got to like the things that she disliked before just because she hadn't tried them. Now I wonder if I can keep the promise of secrecy that I've given. But there's the two ladies. Oh, oh, I've already got a pain in my side as if there's a hole starting to open up.

SCENE 3

(Leonora; Laurentia; Pernille)

LEONORA. Don't you think the same as I do, sister, that Mother isn't like she was before she went away?

LAURENTIA. Yes, I do.

LEONORA. She spent half an hour this morning prinking and painting herself.

LAURENTIA. And I found a novel instead of a prayer-book on her table.

LEONORA. But look at Pernille standing there with her head drooping. Heark'ee, Pernille, why are you so distracted?

PERNILLE. I'm not well, Miss.

LEONORA. What's the matter?

PERNILLE. I'm going to have a child.

LEONORA. What a misfortune! You're going to have a child?

PERNILLE. Yes, and what's more, it's almost ready to be born. It's a deformed child that has to come out of my side.

LEONORA. But that's an enigma. What does it mean?

PERNILLE. It means I'm going round ready to give birth to a secret that I must not tell.

LEONORA. But can you keep anything a secret from us? Tell us what it is.

PERNILLE. Oh, I can't hold it in any longer. Your mother—

LEONORA. What d'you want to tell us about mother?

PERNILLE. Nothing very much, Miss, except that she's gone quite crazy since she took that trip.

LEONORA. But we haven't noticed any signs of madness.

PERNILLE. Maybe you haven't talked with her.

LEONORA. Only for a little last night when she got back and we congratulated her on coming home safely.

PERNILLE. I see you don't know very much.

LEONORA. We only noticed she looked rather merry and gay, and we don't understand why.

PERNILLE. Was that all? That's not enough.

LEONORA. My sister and I were also surprised to see that this morning, instead of singing hymns as usual, she spent an hour at her toilette painting and prinking herself.

PERNILLE. Was that all? It's not enough.

LEONORA. We think it is enough.

PERNILLE. You must do better than that.

LEONORA. I can't believe that an old lady like that would want to get married.

PERNILLE. That's not enough, Miss. You must do better still.

LEONORA. The deuce take you and your better still. That's the worst that could happen—disgrace for her and misfortune for her children.

PERNILLE. I say "better still, better still."

LEONORA. Maybe she wants to marry a definite person here to get social rank. Those pious people and catechizing sisters are usually very keen on their social position.

PERNILLE. Better still, better still.

LEONORA. I don't think she'd marry to get more money, and that old Jeronimus, who—

PERNILLE. Old Jeronimus? Bad cess to him! Is that a match for a gracious young woman like your mother?

LEONORA. Do you call her young when she's between fifty and sixty?

PERNILLE. Your mother's not more than twenty.

LEONORA. And her youngest daughter is seventeen.

PERNILLE. That doesn't matter, Miss. In this matter you've got to forget about reason and put arithmetic to one side. A lady who is crazy about men and runs after young officers so as to marry one of them cannot be old, although she's quite gray or bald.

LEONORA. What? Does she want to marry a young officer?

LAURENTIA. Perhaps she's looking for a young officer for me.

PERNILLE. No, Miss Laurentia. Don't deceive yourself. It's for herself, and the man will be your stepfather.

LAURENTIA. If you're joking, you'll be sorry for it.

PERNILLE. I swear by all that's holy, it's quite true. Look here: these ducats were given to me by your mother so that I'd help her or at least say nothing until she had carried out her plan. And she's going to use the services of Madame Kirsten the matchmaker, who usually helps people in love. To stop this I must go off at once to that marriage-broker and promise her a good reward if she can find some way to prevent this misfortune. Goodbye for now. You just go away.

Scene 4

(Terentia, with a mirror in her hand)

I ought to get hold of old Kirsten today, wherever she is. *(Looks in the mirror.)* I needn't be afraid. 'Pon my soul there's still some traces of beauty in my face. I'm really pleased with my eyes, and if the mirror doesn't deceive me, they can make even a young beau excited. The longer I look at myself, the more pleasing my features seem to be. If I didn't have that one deucedly big wrinkle in my forehead, I should be thought a beauty. But of course a dowry of thirty thousand rix-dollars can make a wrinkle invisible to a young suitor, and the praise that Madame Kirsten will give me can settle everything. I sent her a message but she wasn't at home. However, her servants promised to send her here as soon as she came home. *(She continues to look at herself in the mirror, smiling all the time.)*

Scene 5

(Kirsten the matchmaker, who is an actress in disguise; Terentia)

Kirsten. On the way here Pernille told me a confoundedly funny story. I must help these poor young ladies. They've promised me a good fee for my trouble. I've a plot already in my head that I can carry out. Pernille has a sister with a beautiful face and a good shape. I've told her to disguise this sister quickly as an officer and suitor. I'll look after the rest. But there's the lady looking at herself in a mirror. What the devil! She's covered with paint and powder. I must keep my face straight and encourage her plans, so as to work out my plot. Welcome home, dear lady! How did you get on during your trip?

Terentia. I never had a more pleasant journey.

Kirsten. I see too that you are well both physically and mentally; everything about you seems bright and cheerful.

TERENTIA. I've never been in a better humor in all my life.

KIRSTEN. You look as if you are engaged and are going to be married.

TERENTIA. I'm very happy to hear that.

KIRSTEN. I'faith I can't take my eyes off you, you look so lovely from top to toe.

TERENTIA. But tell me frankly, Madame, without any flattery, what do you think of my features?

KIRSTEN. I can assure you that everything follows beauty's laws.

TERENTIA. I'm very pleased to hear that, as I know you are an expert on beauty. But that's something I can't boast about; it's Heaven's doing.

KIRSTEN. Good gracious, what sparkling eyes, what a straight nose, what lovely cheeks!

TERENTIA. But do you think that wrinkle on my forehead can spoil me?

KIRSTEN. On the contrary, I think it's an ornament; it makes your face look manly and majestic.

TERENTIA. I think my figure will do.

KIRSTEN. Will you please turn round, Madame? *(Terentia turns towards the right.)* Good gracious, what a figure! Will you please turn the other side? *(Terentia turns to the left.)* I call that a complete figure; you look as if you were laced. Now turn your third side.

TERENTIA. I only have two sides.

KIRSTEN. That's quite right, but I wish you had more. You can't have too much of what is so beautiful.

TERENTIA. Heark'ee, Madame. I've noticed that several young beaus have their eyes on me. If I decided to make one of them happy, could people say anything bad about me?

KIRSTEN. Certainly not. Far from advising you not to, I'd rather tell you to do it.

TERENTIA. Then I can tell you my plan. I've really made up my mind to look for a husband.

KIRSTEN. That's a very good thing to do, Madame. Why should you torment yourself by remaining a lonely widow any longer?

TERENTIA. And it must be a lively young beau.

KIRSTEN. The younger the better; young flesh is always better than old.

TERENTIA. No one can help me better than you; you know most of the young fellows here.

KIRSTEN. If you tell me, Madame, what sort of person you want, I'll see if I have anyone on my list that would please you.

TERENTIA. He must be a military man, between twenty and thirty. He must be good-looking and adaptable. It doesn't matter if he has no money or if he is inclined to be jealous; that would mean he is pleased with my appearance.

KIRSTEN *(mumbling over her list)*. Good heavens, here's just the right person! Look. Number five, Captain Frands von Fraulieb, twenty-four years old, with a face like a girl and a good figure. He's pleasant and adaptable and is jealous of the person he's in love with.

TERENTIA. Good gracious, my blood's beginning to boil over! But where can I find him?

KIRSTEN. He's staying in my house, so I know exactly what he's like.

TERENTIA. You don't think he'll refuse me, Madame?

KIRSTEN. Why should he refuse a lady who has both beauty and wealth? Besides, he takes my advice about everything. Just let me look after this.

TERENTIA. Come, let's go inside a little while to think it over further.

SCENE 6

(Leonora; Laurentia; Pernille)

LEONORA. Now we'll hear what Pernille has arranged with the old lady. But there she is. Pernille, how are things going?

PERNILLE. I only know the beginning of the plot and not

what she intends. All she has said is that I should dress my sister Elsebet in an officer's uniform and she'll do the rest.

LAURENTIA. But isn't it a shame to make a fool of one's mother?

PERNILLE. She's making a fool of herself. We're only trying to cure her foolishness.

LEONORA. That's quite true. When words and warnings don't help, you must drive out folly by folly.

LAURENTIA. But is Mama really so silly?

PERNILLE. What a question! Can you say that a lady between fifty and sixty years old who runs after young beaus shows the least sign of common sense?

LEONORA. She really does seem to have a screw loose, for—

PERNILLE. I don't know how many screws there are in a person's brain, but Madame Terentia seems to have them all loose.

LEONORA. But, Pernille, how can a person change so quickly and so much? Hasn't the devil something to do with it?

PERNILLE. People always bring in the devil when they want an excuse for anything. That's what the girl said who was going to have a baby: "Look at what the devil can do!" It's quite natural for a person to go from one extreme to another, and there are lots of examples of decent old pussies being changed into frisky calves.

LEONORA. But surely there must have been some reason for such a funny change.

PERNILLE. Of course there was a reason. Your mother, when she was in the capital, got into amusing company which she hadn't known before and began to get a taste for it and so wanted to change her previously strict way of life, but as she couldn't check herself, the medicine was worse than the sickness.

LEONORA. Do you think then that her former piety was put on?

PERNILLE. I can't say exactly, but I know that several pious people have lapsed in the same way, so it's best to be moderate in everything. But there's Madame Kirsten coming with the suitor who has fallen in love and is going to be your stepfather.

Scene 7

(Kirsten; Elsebet, disguised, with a gold-laced uniform and a hat with ostrich feathers; the people of the previous scene)

Pernille. Ha, ha, who the devil would know you in that dress, Elsebet?

Elsebet. Speak more respectfully when you speak to a captain.

Pernille. Are you really a captain?

Elsebet. Can't you see that by my uniform, my walk, and my looks?

Pernille. I see you'll play your part quite well. But, Madame Kirsten, what is going to happen?

Kirsten. She's going to pretend to woo Madame Terentia.

Pernille. But what will come of it?

Kirsten. I can't tell you just now; leave the rest to me. Heark'ee, Elsebet, you mustn't pretend to be too deeply in love; be a little cool. That will make her all the more eager.

Elsebet. I'll play my part well enough, don't be afraid.

Kirsten. There's the lady coming—go off to one side.

Scene 8

(Kirsten; Terentia, dressed up in a ridiculous way; Elsebet)

Kirsten *(to Elsebet)*. Just stay at this end while I tell the lady you are here.

Terentia. Dear Madame Kirsten, have you managed to do anything for me?

Kirsten. Everything's going well. I've persuaded the party to come along here so that he can make a good impression.

Terentia. I suppose he's seen me before.

KIRSTEN. Of course he's seen you and he likes your appearance, so that I feel there'll be no difficulty.

TERENTIA. But why didn't you bring him here at once?

KIRSTEN. Will you please look to the left without showing you are doing so?

TERENTIA. Good gracious, is that him standing over there? He's a dainty tidbit; no painter could—

KIRSTEN *(drawing her to one side)*. Gently, gently, dear lady! You must be very proper and act a little cold or else you'll spoil everything.

TERENTIA. But if I am too cold, won't I spoil it?

KIRSTEN. You mustn't be too cold but just show the decency that is expected from our sex.

TERENTIA. I'll follow your advice as best I can.

KIRSTEN *(to Elsebet)*. Will the gracious captain please come a little nearer? May I introduce the beautiful and virtuous lady whose acquaintance you wished to make?

ELSEBET *(to Terentia)*. Will the gracious lady forgive me for taking the liberty of paying my respects to her? I wouldn't have dared if this good Madame Kirsten, who is my landlady, had not told me that—

TERENTIA. You need not apologize, Captain. I can assure you that the first sight of your person—

KIRSTEN *(to Terentia in a low voice)*. Gently, gently, dear lady! You're going too fast.

TERENTIA. I can assure you, sir, that I must respect anyone who has been promoted so quickly in the army.

ELSEBET. Thank you for the kind thoughts you have about me. Though I'm still young, I've fought in four great battles in Flanders.

TERENTIA. Four great battles?

ELSEBET. Yes, four great battles and a bit of a fifth. If my sword could speak, it would bear witness to my conduct in those actions. But it's not right for me to praise myself. All I can say is that I've tried to do my duty.

Kirsten. Everybody knows about the captain's bravery and gallant conduct both in peace and war. That's why everyone respects and loves him. And it's strange that although he's always shown a sort of coolness to women, they are very fond of him.

Terentia. Have you a natural dislike of marriage, Captain?

Elsebet. I can't say that. There might easily be someone who could win my heart.

Terentia. What sort of person would that be?

Elsebet. Speaking without flattery, she ought to be a person with the qualities you possess, Madame.

Terentia. I thank your honor for the kind thoughts you have about me. I must also open my heart to you and confess—

Kirsten *(to Terentia, drawing her to one side)*. 'Pon my soul, you are going too fast, Madame.

Terentia. I was saying that you could attract me more than anyone else if I decided to change my condition, but—

Elsebet. Oh, that "but" pierces my heart.

Terentia. My late lamented husband means so much to me that I can never forget him.

Elsebet. Then I see I must go away disconsolate, but since fate will have it so, permit me, as I leave, to kiss your hand and ask for your pure friendship. *(Kisses her hand and exits.)*

Kirsten *(running after him)*. Here, doesn't a soldier like you know that a fort will not give in at the first shot? Don't be so hasty; have a little patience. Let me talk to the lady a little more. *(To Terentia.)* My dear lady, it's all right, you can be quite calm.

Terentia *(softly to Kirsten)*. My whole body's shivering and shaking. Your precautions have nearly lost me my catch.

Kirsten. Let's talk quite frankly. I know your disposition, Madame, and I can see from your face and looks that the captain hasn't made this trip for nothing. Then speak, Madame, and don't be insincere. Will you let this gentleman go away disconsolate?

TERENTIA. If it's Heaven's will, I'll grant his request.

KIRSTEN. I won't swear it's the will of Heaven. Very well, take each other's hand without any more fuss. *(She takes their hands and places them together.)*

KIRSTEN. Now, Captain, you must go home at once and tell your friends what Heaven has decided, and the lady must also tell her daughters.

ELSEBET *(kissing Terentia's hand)*. Goodbye for now, my dearest.

TERENTIA. Farewell, sweet angel, and come back as soon as you can.

SCENE 9

(Kirsten; Terentia)

KIRSTEN. Oh, oh, I can't keep from crying.

TERENTIA. Why are you crying, Madame?

KIRSTEN. It's just from joy; I'm so touched by this happy union I was fortunate enough to arrange. I've used my services to arrange a lot of marriages in my day, but none of them has pleased me so much as this one. It's a pure, genuine, disinterested and extraordinary love. There aren't many matches like it. Now I must leave you for a little, while you talk to your children and satisfy them in case they have any objection to the match. *(Exit.)*

SCENE 10

(Terentia; Leonora; Laurentia; Pernille)

TERENTIA. Come out here, children. I've got something to tell you. Listen, dear daughters. It's no use for me to stay single any more. I must have a man to look after my house, and I've already arranged to marry one who will be a good stepfather to you.

PERNILLE. Then you haven't thought very long about it, Madame. You only got home yesterday and you're already engaged today. *(The daughters cry.)*

TERENTIA. Don't cry, children. Tears won't help.

PERNILLE. If crying helped, we'd keep on till the house was flooded.

TERENTIA. It's done now. I've given my promise, and I can't break it.

PERNILLE. May I ask you, Madame, who is the bridegroom?

TERENTIA. He's a fine young beau, Captain Frands von Fraulieb. I wonder if you know him?

PERNILLE. Of course I know him. He's really most suitable for your youngest daughter Laurentia, Madame.

LAURENTIA. I'faith Pernille's right about that.

TERENTIA. You'll get a husband all right. You're still too young to marry.

PERNILLE. And you are too old, Madame. So let your eldest daughter have him.

TERENTIA. No, thank you! I'll certainly keep him myself. It must be; it's the will of Heaven.

PERNILLE. Is it the will of Heaven that an old lady with grown-up daughters should spoil their chances by marrying a young coxcomb? I can't understand that sort of religion.

TERENTIA. It's true he's young, but he has the virtue and sense of an old man. They praise him everywhere both in town and in the army, and it's known that he's already shown how brave he is in four battles.

PERNILLE. Is that why you want him—because he knows how to handle his sword? I should have thought you'd want some different qualities.

TERENTIA. Just keep quiet, Pernille. It's no use talking. Don't you remember what you promised me?

PERNILLE. I promised more than I can do.

TERENTIA. Let me speak to my daughters alone. What do you say, children? Are you going to rise up against your mother?

LEONORA. Not at all, Mama. We must be quiet and put up with it.

TERENTIA. But what's all that noise and crying out in the hall? Run out and see what's the matter.

PERNILLE. It's Madame Kirsten the matchmaker, bathed in tears.

TERENTIA. Let her come in.

SCENE II

(Kirsten; the characters from the previous scene)

KIRSTEN. Oh, such a terrible thing has happened!

TERENTIA. What is it?

KIRSTEN. Such a sad story!

TERENTIA. Tell me what it is; I'm trembling all over.

KIRSTEN. It's just like what happened in Jutland in my grandmother's day.

TERENTIA. What is it, Madame? I'm dying to know.

KIRSTEN. It happened just on the same occasion as this, so it's clear that Heaven is against it.

TERENTIA. Don't torment me any more; tell me at once.

KIRSTEN. Oh, what a wretched woman I am, to be mixed up with such a wicked business! Oh, oh, oh—

TERENTIA. What business? Tell me, in the devil's name!

KIRSTEN. I'll tell you the story, if my tears and sighs will allow me. Madame, the young captain—

TERENTIA. What's happened to him?

KIRSTEN. I tell you, the young captain— Oh, I can't say any more, oh, oh, oh—

TERENTIA. That doesn't tell me anything.

KIRSTEN. I'm telling you, the young captain— oh, oh, oh— Wait a little, let me get my breath. The young captain— He had just got up to his room when I heard him shout at the top of his voice. When I asked him what had happened, he said in a high voice: "Dear Madame, tell me who I am. I felt a pain and had a fright and now I find that everything in me is changed, both my mind and my body. I have different feelings, a different voice, different limbs, a different soul." I at once thought he had gone crazy, but when my sister and I remembered the story from Jutland and some others like it that we'd read in reliable papers, and went in to investigate the whole thing, we found that he—oh, oh, oh—

TERENTIA. What did you find?

KIRSTEN. That he had changed from a captain to a young girl. *(They all cry out.)*

PERNILLE. Oh— A young girl, did you say?

KIRSTEN. Yes, a young girl; all the neighborhood knows it. Jacob the schoolteacher is sitting there now comforting her, as she's quite desperate. *(They all cry out again.)* My sister is putting women's clothes on her at once and has promised to bring her here, to show there's no doubt about it.

PERNILLE. Is there nothing left of her previous appearance?

KIRSTEN. Only her face. *(They all cry out.)* The schoolteacher told us of several examples of miracles like it; I think he called them metamorphoses. But look, there she is in her girl's dress. *(They all cry out again.)*

SCENE 12

(Elsebet, crying; the rest)

KIRSTEN. Oh, what a sight! It will break my heart. Come nearer, dear Captain, and tell the lady how it all happened.

ELSEBET. I don't own that title. I know my fate now. My weapons now are the spinning-wheel and the tea-things.

KIRSTEN. What do you think of this, Madame?

TERENTIA. I must believe my eyes. I'm so frightened and ashamed that I can't speak. I only blame my foolishness and vanity, ask pardon of my children, and for the rest of my life in my single state I'll try to lament the sin I've committed. As for you, my dear girl, who have suffered this misfortune, be patient about it and be content with your fate, and think how much greater your punishment might have been.

PERNILLE. Yes, it certainly might; there are cases of people who were turned into werewolves.

ELSEBET. Yes, I'll be patient and take the warning to heart.

She comes forward and sings:

You women and girls
You must not be too sad.
What's done can't be changed,
Take the good with the bad.
I suppose it's your loss,
But each lass gets her mate,
For of lads there are plenty,
Both early and late.

They all repeat this.

PERNILLE *(as she leaves the stage, sings)*:

A merry play has been performed
  With actresses alone.
By this and many other things
  We hope that we have shown
It's not so hard to carry on
  Without a single man,
For girls and women play their parts
  As ably as men can.

They all repeat this.

COMMITTEE ON PUBLICATIONS
THE AMERICAN-SCANDINAVIAN FOUNDATION

Professor William Witherle Lawrence
Columbia University

Dr. Henry Goddard Leach
The American-Scandinavian Foundation

Mr. Holger Lundbergh
The American-Swedish News Exchange

Professor Kemp Malone
The Johns Hopkins University

Mr. Frederick Schaefer
Carnegie Institute of Technology

Professor Hamilton M. Smyser
Connecticut College for Women

Dr. John B. C. Watkins
Canadian Department of External Affairs